REBIRTH

The Spiritual Evolution that Reunited Two Souls

By Lisa C. Arrington

Edited by Candace Johnson
Cover art by Molly Chopin
Cover design by Adam Hay
Photographs by Lisa Arrington

ISBN: 979-8-218-96106-0

Website: https://etherealsoul.net/

Dedication & Acknowledgments

This book is dedicated to you, who dances to the rhythm of life's inaudible song.

Mentioned in this book:

Irina Nola (Past Life Regression Therapist)
https://www.neworleanshypnosis.com/

Emily Maples (Psychic Reader)
Raleigh, NC

"The universe always puts us back together... <u>Always</u>."
— Gregory Alan Bowler

Reviews & Testimonials

"This book has made a big impact on my journey, and consequently, for many others in the future. So much of it is telling my story since my twin flame passed over. Rebirth is a game changer." — Jenna T.

"The story has truly touched me. I can relate 100%. I was with my soul-mate for 33 years before she died recently. I was seeing number patterns daily leading up to her death and have since. I strangely knew that somehow we would be parted but my ego hoped that we would make the grade together and would walk forward in a new earth. This has helped me make sense of a difficult time in my life." — Greg N.

"There are many stories pertaining to Twin Flames, but since reading this one, I have felt my Twin Flame connection grow stronger. That's incredible! It has inspired me to connect with him every day now and led to more intense communication and manifestations." — Heather R.

"Reading your book gives me shivers and brings tears to my eyes. It is captivating, beautifully written. These are messages that many in the world could use right now, and overall the intentions and lessons of this story resonate so deeply with me." — Molly C.

"I can't even begin to tell you how cathartic reading Rebirth has been. My stomach is stirring with all these emotions that have been lying dormant since my Twin Flame died! This book is amazing and will help so many souls." — Sam K.

"I've found it, a story that resonates with my own. I've been searching for something to relate to. The way Rebirth is written was like me telling what's happened to me, almost event to event. Thank you for sharing your story." — Fawn

Contents

Preface

Humankind has long been fascinated by the unseen things that connect us—the forces of the "psychic" or *energetic* side of life. This metaphysical world exists alongside the physical world, connecting our consciousness to our bodies and our bodies to one another. It is the source of the universal connection we strive to tap into.

If you're captivated by the mystical yet scientific world of energy and feel there's something more to this life, then it's a pleasure to connect with you.

By picking up this book, a connection has formed between us in the ether. This connection can be wielded as a powerful tool for your personal development and the evolution of the spirit that inhabits your being.

My intention is that this story opens you to a world of new possibilities. I pray that the words in this book resonate with you and bring healing and grace.

Expand your perspective to one of new heights. See how love is an *energetic* exchange that extends beyond life situational circumstances or physical proximity to others.

Like the energetic exchange of love, the soul connection that has been dubbed, "Twin Flames," transcends space, time, and preconceived boundaries of the universe.

It was in the early 2000s when I first met my Twin Flame, Gregory—my greatest love. Our time together followed the typical progression of a Twin Flame relationship. The runner-chaser stage, separation stage, and so on. That is, until he unexpectedly passed away on January 22, 2021.

To my surprise, although he had physically left this world, our journey was far from over. A groundbreaking promise came through to me and was intuitively marked on my heart: I would find him again. We would continue along our path.

This promise of rebirth sparked a newfound hope—hope that I would one day feel the warmth and comfort of being in the presence of the one I loved again. However, the idea that I would meet someone with my late loved one's energy defied all logic.

Before I could wrap my head around this crazy notion, I'd have to first resolve the egging questions. How could my partner leave me behind all alone? How could I still feel his presence as strongly as if he was here? Was there something more to the seemingly non-stop flow of synchronicities and messages coming through?

My initial search for answers was disappointing. The information about navigating the Twin Flame journey after one person had passed was severely lacking. The material available was subpar and didn't offer sufficient answers. This sentiment was shared by others like me, made obvious on forums and message boards for those who'd lost their Twin Flame.

There was a need for more useful information. I realized I was experiencing a real-life story that could help fill that need. I immediately went to work and spent over two years documenting and researching everything I could related to this journey.

As a Search Engine Optimization (SEO) manager in my professional life, I analyze a wide array of information from user behavior and search trends, to data relevance models and entity relationships in Artificial Intelligence (AI), to the hundreds of ranking factors that search engine algorithms rely on. I applied this polymathic approach to uncover meaningful connections across different modalities and topics like bereavement, healing, and spirituality.

My investigation revealed a network of people who are guided by an altruistic purpose to aid in humanity's evolution from the third dimension to fifth dimension; from Old Earth to New Earth; and from the Age of Pisces to the Age of Aquarius. Everything I uncovered pointed to life's beautiful orchestration playing out in divine timing.

When deciding if I should write this book, I was hesitant. I thought, *"Who am I to produce such copy?"* As I struggled with this sentiment of self-doubt, I received an email from someone who'd found the blog version of this story on my website. They asked if it was available in print format (aka a book).

My jaw dropped. What are the odds that this happened at the exact time I needed assurance to make my decision? It was the universe's way of confirming which direction I should take. This type of highly connected awareness—the ability to expand your senses to recognize patterns and derive deeper meanings—is the awesome potential of spiritual evolution.

This book is designed to facilitate that spiritual evolution. It is meant to heighten conscious awareness. Take note of any synchronicities you see along the way. Consider the salience of my story to yours. Remember, *everything is connected*.

What Are Twin Flames?

The phrase "Twin Flames" or "Twin Souls" describes a unique type of spiritual connection between two people. While a person can have multiple *soulmates* to help them learn lessons or aid in a certain cycle of their life, a person has only one spiritual match who is their *Twin Flame*. Twin Flames are here to facilitate humanity's spiritual evolution and usher in an expanded, limitless expression of love.

When the two Twin Flame partners come together, it's an incredibly powerful experience marked by an energy exchange or activation that's both exhilarating and overwhelming. They feel an unmistakably deep and intuitive recognition of one another's energy, so strongly that it's as if they've known each other before.

Because the partners resonate with the same frequency, it causes an undeniable *magnetism* between them. But when you face two magnets of the same polarity together, they don't stick—they repel one another.

Through the stages of their journey, the partners grow to shed what no longer serves them, effectively changing their polarity to attract one another rather than to resist. This is why the Twin Flame relationship is known to be particularly challenging: the partners must work through their ego, past trauma, and old beliefs, all while trying to share a healthy relationship.

It can be a bumpy road, but the reward is worth it. The ultimate goal of Twin Flames is to fulfill their higher mission of bringing *universal love* (aka unconditional love) to the world. They teach us to challenge the boundaries of the impossible (aka *I'm possible*).

What's fascinating about Twin Flames is that both partners do not need to be physically here on Earth to work their journey together because they are connected by something called the silver cord. This cord, which is mentioned in ancient text and scripture, such as the Bible, is a metaphysical link that tethers the pair across realms, regardless of the illusion of separation that many of us perceive in spatial reality.

Such a connection transcends space and time and defies traditional beliefs of life and death. It challenges the concept that one soul equals one body. It supports an understanding that we are spiritual beings having a physical experience, and are capable of tapping into the metaphysical current that binds us to the ones we love.

This story will show how you can follow the path of connection and reach the frequency of miracles in your own life. When you hear spirit's call, the lessons of *Rebirth* will encourage you to embrace the full potential of what you're being promised, as your intuition will never lead you astray.

The Setup

The love of my life, my Twin Flame, just died. You'd think I'd be overrun with grief, paralyzed by the pain of my loss, and crushed by a massive depression that extended to the very depths of my soul. But funny enough, I wasn't.

I tried to mourn him but each time I was met with an overflowing sense of infinite love. It was the opposite of what I thought I should've been feeling. Why wasn't I experiencing the gut-wrenching pain of having my loved one ripped away? Was something wrong with me?

Things got even crazier when I couldn't shake the feeling that I'd see him again in *this* life. It was more than a feeling. It was an intuitive promise of rebirth, permanently marked on my heart. Though I didn't yet understand how it'd come to be, I had faith we would reunite.

Gregory died from an accidental overdose on January 22, 2021 while in the recovery process. The rapid development of potent, Narcan-resistant opioids that were plaguing the street at the height of the Coronavirus pandemic and his dampened will to keep fighting the good fight created a window of opportunity for his soul to return to Spirit.

I was a newly separated single mother from a previous relationship with a full-time job and a four-year-old daughter. The endings, transformations, and beginnings in nearly every aspect of my life at the time, including Greg's passing, signaled that things were setting up for a whole new chapter.

I didn't know how to properly channel the ocean of intense intuitive feelings and synchronistic evidence coming through. I wasn't well-versed in spirit communication, past lives, or psychic mediumship. I couldn't help but feel I was being presented with an opportunity to co-create my very own miracle. I *could* reunite with my loved one.

Convinced that I was either crazy from grieving or witnessing a true miracle in the making, I wasted no time in getting to work. However, it seemed that no one had a good grasp on the topic of death and rebirth in Twin Flames. Not spiritual teachers, internet articles, message boards, or acclaimed psychics and mediums. I'd have to learn to sharpen my senses and rely on my intuition to find the answers myself.

I dove headfirst into doing energy sessions, meditations, Reiki healing, and more. I explored theories of quantum physics and multidimensional science. I strengthened my foundation in my faith and meticulously studied biblical scripture. I did anything and everything to expand my boundaries and heal.

In my research, the idea that Twin Flame couples were "one soul, two bodies" became problematic. Sharing a soul with your significant other sounds nice at first. Who *wouldn't* want to feel that dreamy, intoxicating feeling of being divinely connected to your one and only, meant-to-be partner? The theory of Twin Flames being "one soul, two bodies" quickly falls apart when you consider the complexity of the universe and how our souls are created with this same complexity. *Every* soul has multiple incarnations or bodies stemming from their Higher Self energy.

Twin Flames are said to share the same Higher Self or be of the same Oversoul. Imagine a hierarchical chart with the Oversoul an Higher Self at the top—the highest levels of your spirit. From there, your spirit branches out into groups of monadic soul energy, which then branch out into multiple incarnations or personalities.

This would mean that *everyone* is a "split soul" or a fragment of their larger soul, in one way or another.

This new understanding supported my hope that I'd encounter another fragment of Greg's soul again. It didn't mean that Greg would magically rematerialize from the grave. It meant that I'd find his soul in a new individual who resonates the same energy that Greg had.

Contrary to the belief that the soul enters a body at birth, there are accounts of the soul entering the body of a person who's already living.

In India, a man reported that he could remember the instance of his soul entering his body when he was three years old; not at birth.

I remember feeling the sensation of my soul coming into my twenty-seven-year-old body during a near-death experience. So, I knew it was possible for my Twin Flame's soul to incarnate or activate in another person at a time other than birth.

That explained the soul part, but there were still so many questions to answer.

I wanted to understand:

- If the goal of Twin Flames is to be in Union, how could Greg die and leave me in a state of separation?
- How could I still feel his energy so strongly?
- Why were synchronicities occurring seemingly everywhere I looked?
- Were these experiences real or figments of my imagination caused by grief?
- Were there other people like me? Did other Twin Flame widow/widowers feel the same conviction that their loved one would return?

I spent the next two years documenting the journey of rebirth. I kept journals and files to track everything from messages in meditation to visions in dreams and supernatural encounters. I documented every occurrence no matter how big or small, profound or trivial, material or metaphysical.

Trusting in the Process

Whenever I started to doubt that what I was receiving was true, the universe would do something to quell my doubt. Each time sending a bigger, more pronounced, more profound sign than before. This reinforced my trust in the process and the belief that the universe always has my back.

For instance, when I published parts of my journey on a small blog that included a contact form to reach me, the very first message I received was from a man named Greg. Of all the names in the world, the person's name was *Greg*—the name of my late Twin Flame. That's the kind of thing you couldn't make up if you tried!

This man's partner died on October 1, 2021. Mine died on January 22, 2021. Written in a date format, that's 10/01/2021 and 01/22/2021. These dates share numerical synchronicity in the ones and twos or twelve—the divine number that represents completion and harmonic balance in the cosmic order. This point of connection between these two dates is an example of an *embedding*.

In machine learning and AI, an embedding is a representation of an object or word. It's used to derive meaning and create an understanding of the object in relation to other things. In life, metaphorical embeddings, such as numerical synchronicities in dates and times, are all around us. They exist to help us understand the events in our lives in relation to ourselves, which in turn helps us understand and define ourselves on a deeper level. When you document these embeddings, they form meaningful patterns and trends over time.

Like the man who messaged me, everyone fantasizes about their loved one being alive again. But the divine promise of rebirth is not to be confused with wishful thinking. True rebirth requires transformation. It asks you to completely let go of the person you once knew to make space for their new form.

Letting go heals and expands one's consciousness—aspects of the spiritual development that fuel humanity's ascension. So you see, this isn't a love story about Twin Flames. It's a love story about humanity.

A 5D Relationship in a 3D World

The passing of a Twin Flame serves as an activation for the surviving partner. They learn to value their late partner's metaphysical energy as much as they valued their physical body. No longer able to see their partner's presence in the 3D material realm, their focus shifts to the energetic presence they feel from their partner in Spirit (Spirit is sometimes referred to as the 5D. Note that the fourth dimension is skipped because 4D is the dimension of time).

Now that their partner exists in Spirit only, they're free to experience their partner's essence in its truest form. Their partner isn't confined to the boundaries of a human vessel anymore. The fable that's been told to them all their lives that physical individuality equals "separation" is shattered. They see through this illusion of disconnection and learn that they are never truly separated. Their connection is always primed and accessible.

This happened to Sarah, a Twin Flame widow who lost her husband after three decades of marriage and three children together. Sarah reached out to me after reading my story on my website. She told me of her loss and journey to work with her late husband's energy to discover a greater purpose within herself.

Though her husband had died unexpectedly, the larger-than-life love that bonded their souls cut through her grief like a hot knife through butter. Sarah chose to forgo dwelling on her physical loss and home in on the special connection that remained. She could feel her husband was still with her, and he reminded her of this every day.

Sarah went to a local psychic in her area for a reading. The psychic revealed that her husband, her Twin Flame, had been in her life to provide her with her three children. He had fulfilled his purpose of coming into the world and was free to exit at the time of his death—thus explaining his passing.

This knowledge helped Sarah appreciate her Twin Flame in his Spirit form and put aside her desire for her family to be defined by external pressures and definitions of what a family unit *should* look like. She dispelled the notion that she must search for a partner to serve as a father figure to her kids so that she could live her life in its full meaning and purpose.

The story of how Sarah lost her Twin Flame and the circumstances surrounding their connection catapulted her onto a path she otherwise wouldn't have been able to reach without his sacrifice. It's a touching story of how the Twin Flame journey doesn't end when one partner passes on.

You can continue to work with your loved one's energy from your seat in the 3D. You're able to access a life of love and connection, even if your loved one has passed away or you're made to believe you are less than you truly are. You are *always* capable of tapping into the metaphysical fabric that connects us. It shows how stunningly limitless life really is.

I learned to understand this in my own journey. So that you get the gravity of the signs and synchronicities that appear and understand the *why* behind the concepts mentioned, let's go back to the beginning of this story of rebirth to the first time I met my Twin Flame.

Chapter 1

Beginning the Twin Flame Journey

I met Greg when I was eighteen. We orbited the same social circles and had crossed each other's paths a few times but never interacted or were formally introduced. In those days, the cutting-edge tech to talk online was AOL Instant Messenger (AIM). Greg got my info from a friend and sent me an instant message (IM) from his screen name, "calisurferboy." I couldn't help but see the vanity in his handle, as if he idolized California and tried to apply the coolness of it to himself.

His attitude was playful and flirtatious. He had a suave, clever tone that screamed, "There's no one like me. I'm unlike anyone you've ever met." But his attempts to get my attention went unnoticed. I wrote them off as just another guy trying his luck with whatever girl he could get to reply. Though that was my thinking then, it wouldn't be long before I wasn't able to forget him. We were energetically calling each other into our lives, long before either of us realized it.

When Greg and I finally did meet formally, my world changed. Reality itself shifted in a powerful moment of electric connection. I'd never felt anything like this energy activation, and I wouldn't again until the day he passed away thirteen years later.

The Activation

It was a warm summer night, and my boyfriend, Brandon, and I were on our way to a house party. It was weighing on my mind that someone with the screen name "calisurferboy" had sent me an IM earlier that day. They claimed that they knew me and were a friend of Brandon's. With a few minutes to kill on the car ride to the party, I asked Brandon if he knew who this "calisurferboy" was.

"You know Greg," he said, as he tried to refresh my memory with times we'd all hung out. But nothing rang a bell.

We arrived at the party right as the sun was setting. It was a picturesque North Carolina evening. The glow of the fireflies popped off the twilight-lit landscape as we walked toward the house. The front door was open to welcome attendees. With my gaze set on the entrance, I saw Greg framed in the open doorway, almost like it was divinely timed. Brandon reached his arm out and pointed.

"*That's* him," he said.

A bright fluorescent light from inside the house created a backlit effect around Greg's figure. The scene looked like something from an angelic vision.

I was both surprised and relieved to find that the person who'd been IMing me was actually very handsome. The second I lay eyes on him, I felt my skin flush and was overwhelmed with anxious excitement. Greg must've felt my stare because the next thing I realized, he was staring back at me.

The air electrified. A jolting bolt of energy pulsed through my body. The energy of this moment was so powerful that it affected my vision. I could visually see this strong energy activating and reflecting in the world around me.

Though it happened in a split second, time felt as though it had stopped for us. No words were spoken. The information inferred in this moment was unlocked, deeply rooted in our DNA. I'd found my energetic tether in this life... my Twin Flame.

The Ghost Hunt

It wouldn't be long before our paths would cross again. Just a few days later, a group of us were hanging out at a friend's place. None of us felt that we quite fit in with "normal" society. We were each searching for the companionship of others we could relate to. We were the oddballs, the rebels, the deep souls.

At a time when we'd graduated high school but hadn't started college yet, we had no serious responsibilities or obligations. The summer days were ours for the taking. We drank Sparks (an alcoholic energy drink that would be banned in 2008), smoked cigarettes, and thought we were so cool.

One evening, there was a special magic in the air (though it could've also been the lingering scent of marijuana and teenage angst). Somehow, the topic of ghosts came up. Everyone started exchanging ghost stories, paranormal experiences, and urban legends. It created a sense of anticipation among the group. We wanted to witness these things for ourselves. Someone piped up and said they knew of a haunted house... and it was just down the street from where we were.

Our little group of misfits set off on foot to find the haunted house. There were six of us, three boys and three girls, including my then-boyfriend, Brandon, and Greg. After a thirty-minute walk down curvy side roads, we arrived at our destination: an abandoned two-story house. Its white siding was weathered from years of being neglected in the North Carolina humidity. Its dark-green shutters bordered the empty windows, giving it an eerie look. We slowly peered in through the front door, not sure of what we would find. Would there be evil spirits lurking about? Or dangerous squatters? Was the structure even stable enough for us to safely go inside?

The group stayed close together as we walked through the front doorway and ventured inward to the downstairs area. One of the kids wandered off, but the rest of us were too enthralled with the supposed haunted dwelling. On high alert for anything strange, we heard a creaking noise coming from upstairs.

The group got nervous. No one could explain where these weird noises were coming from. We'd made it into the kitchen by this point, which was in the back of the house—far away from the closest known exit (the front door)—when there was a pause in the creepy noises overhead.

"Maybe it's the sound of the old house settling," someone proposed.

"Maybe it's just an animal," someone else said.

A third person chimed in, "You guys... it's gotta be a *ghost!*"

With the idea that ghosts were real freshly planted in our heads, our friend who'd wandered off earlier popped out from a dark, adjoining room. His quick movement and loud "BOO" had us jumping out of our skins! I leapt over across the circle of us and latched onto Greg.

He looked at me with surprise. My boyfriend was standing right next to us. Logic says that I should've gone to him. I also hadn't said more than two words to Greg before and didn't know him personally.

Beyond this look of surprise was his strange sense of satisfaction. It's as if he'd been waiting for this, like he knew it was right for our bodies to be that close. Perhaps my instincts knew this as well, and that's why I chose him as my protector.

The panic subsided, and I quickly came back down to Earth to realize I was gripping Greg. I immediately detached from him and tried to shrug it off as no big deal. But it was hard to ignore the gravity of what'd happened between us. I couldn't deny the magnetic pull that was drawing me toward him.

The Infamous "Magnetic Pull"

Twin Flame partners feel drawn to each other in a way they can't ignore. They act like magnets, but when you face two magnets of the same polarity together, they won't stick. Their polarity is so similar that it creates a force that repels rather than attracts them together.

Because they share the same energy, it can be difficult for Twin Flames to have a functional relationship. All the muck and guck from living a life that doesn't serve them disrupts this magnetism. The partners end up reflecting things in the relationship like emotional baggage, past trauma, and 3D beliefs.

They must work to clear the mirror and change their polarity. Eventually, they can use the mirroring effect in a positive way that supports the greater good.

The First Night

Eager to explore this strange connection, I parted ways with Brandon and accepted Greg's invitation to have a homemade meal at his place. I appreciated his effort to create personal intimacy by cooking for me. A man that can cook is always impressive!

It was the night of June 26, 2008. sat at the dining room table and watched as Greg tried to be smooth and suave while he prepared our meal. We were in that awkward stage where you haven't quite gotten comfortable with each other yet, where you're in your head and hyperconscious of your body language, the words you're saying and wondering if you're asking too many questions, does your breath smell OK, and so on.

He put on some music to ease the nervous tension. I immediately recognized the song from Savage Garden's self-titled album. If you've ever listened to old-school Savage Garden, you know it's heavy with themes of space travel, emotion, and allegory. Anyone who likes that album is bound to have something deeper to them.

Greg rushed to change it, as if he didn't mean to play that track, when I blurted out, "Is that Savage Garden? This was my favorite album when I was little!"

He smiled in relief—his cute, signature smile that was kind of quirky but also adorable and attractive—and the nervous tension in the air dissipated. I felt that I saw a glimpse of the real Greg in that moment, not the act he usually put on to appear confident and sure of himself.

Our time together was only beginning, but already there was something magical between us, something that couldn't be explained with the usual rhetoric or through worldly concepts.

The First Months: The Highs of a Twin Flame Love Story

The first months with Greg were dreamy and whimsical. I attended undergrad out of town, but the 120-mile distance didn't faze our connection. We took turns traveling to see each other on weekends. We'd spend those days tucked away in his room above the garage at his parent's house or in my dorm room. We'd laugh and joke together, be each other's "partner in crime" in shenanigans, and when we became physically intimate, it was like we were accessing another dimension. The rest of the world melted away. Time didn't exist. The only thing that mattered in those moments was that I was in his arms.

Greg and I showed traits of being Twin Flames right out of the gate. We'd manifest things without consciously realizing it. As a joke, we referred to ourselves as a "power couple" because of all the unexplained things that happened when we were together.

We communicated without using words, even when miles apart. We could feel each other's emotions, know what the other was thinking, and grasp insanely deep concepts about the other person like it was hidden knowledge already within us. The synchronicities that surrounded our connection, like how Greg lived off a road called Gregory Drive, also provided a strange sense of assurance that we'd found something extremely special together—something divinely meant to be.

Greg and I were lying together in his room after sharing an explosive expression of intimacy one day. We lay with our heads side-by-side and our feet extending outward in opposite directions, so the only part of our bodies that intersected was our faces.

With our eyes closed, we let go and got lost in our bliss. The serenity we felt overpowered our worldly cares. We paid no mind to the fact that we were lying on the cold, hard floor. It felt so good to enjoy the other's energy. We basked in the amazing feeling of being connected on all levels, physically, mentally, emotionally, and spiritually. No words were spoken so as not to disrupt the meditative flow state we'd found.

"This is the closest we will ever be together," I thought.

This sweet sentiment was followed by a wave of crushing disappointment. I was sad to think that it was impossible for me to be any closer to him than I was then. Two people, who are divinely designed to fit together, were limited by the bounds of their physical bodies. But this was a prime example of the illusion of separation.

The world teaches us to value physical proximity, so I was defining my "closeness" to him in a physical sense and not recognizing that metaphysical proximity can be just as powerful. It was an odd thought for an eighteen-year-old. It stands out to me as a noteworthy moment in our history—a precursor for learning the lesson that our spiritual bodies have the closeness I yearned for our physical bodies to have.

Energetic Abilities of Twin Flames

Twin Flames have heightened psychic (aka *energetic*) abilities. The word "psychic" can sometimes carry a negative connotation or get associated with supernatural hocus pocus, so let's exchange "psychic" for "energetic."

Energetic abilities refer to one's sensory perception of the energy fields of our bodies like electromagnetic, infrared, and the multidimensional levels of our soul. Information is constantly transmitted over these channels. We can infer this information through senses like telepathy, remote viewing, and clairvoyance. The high frequency of love allows us to better sense things on these higher levels.

Love is one of the highest frequencies we can produce organically. Resonating such a high frequency opens us up to the energetic side of the universe and sharpens our abilities.

I'd never been so infatuated with a person as I was with Greg. Every time I saw his name pop up on my phone or I saw him in person, my heart fluttered. With each passing day, I loved him more than I did before. Even when we were fighting or there was distance between us, he was my anchor in this world. My other half. The yin to my yang. The cup to my water. Just the thought of him could make me weak in the knees. The defenses I had to protect my heart were no match for him. He broke right through every wall I built and rendered inert every defense mechanism I had.

From Greg's physical being to his beautiful soul to the connection between us, he had an intoxicating power over me. I was under his spell. I cherished every moment together, almost like a part of me knew that our time would end prematurely. I'd mentally take a picture of each precious second. Something as simple as sitting together on the couch watching TV became meaningful moments to cherish. I'd take in things like how his energy felt, the look on his face, or the way his bangs rested over his eyes and turn it into something sacred and permanent in my heart.

The Rebels

We both rejected having to conform to social norms and expectations of the real world at some level. This teenage-like, rebellious nature made the darker things in life very alluring. We'd ponder things of the occult, debating ridiculous questions like can vampires can become sexually stimulated if they're dead and there's no blood flowing in their bodies?

The music of Nine Inch Nails drove us wild, like audible pheromones were floating through the sound waves when we listened. We watched the movie *Queen of the Damned* countless times (Can we talk about the bathtub scene with Deftones' "Change (In the House of Flies)" playing in the background? Goodness gracious!) and attended the live performances of *The Rocky Horror Picture Show* at our local theater.

Greg had such a beautiful heart that it wasn't possible for him to be led astray by things that usually would send others into a spiraling ocean of despair, like his parents' rocky divorce or feeling like the black sheep of the family. His heart kept him in the light, always focused on what was real and true no matter how bogged down he was by life's usual challenges.

The Wounded Warrior

He carried a real "wounded warrior" energy and used the painful experiences from his past as a driving force to help others. I admired this about him. He had an intrinsic motivation to seek fairness and justice for the people he loved. Later, a past life regression would reveal that trait was embedded in his very soul.

On the outside, Greg presented himself as having tons of self-confidence. He was the epitome of tall, dark, and handsome. He knew he was very attractive, but he carried a sinking darkness of insecurity inside. Something unhealed lurked under the surface of this wounded warrior. Greg's insecurities and struggles with his self-esteem would come to inflict so much damage along our Twin Flame journey.

The Dance of Twin Flame Energy

The energy of Twin Flames is in constant motion. It flows rhythmically between the two partners. The goal is to learn to *balance* the energies in perfect harmony. This can take some years or even decades to master. In the meantime, the energy of the couple ebbs and flows in a polarized dance.

One person leads, and the other follows. When one partner leans in, the other leans out. Whatever the leader does, the movement of the couple is guided in that direction.

The tempo of the dance may change, and the follower becomes the leader, but both people cannot lead at once. Also, one person's misstep can affect the whole couple. If either partner misses a beat, then both people will falter. The key is to balance and flow together in harmony.

This is where Twin Flames see a lot of friction and dysfunction. They're not mindful of the flow of energy between them happening at all times.

Knowing that whatever energy one puts in, the other will have to react to it, Twin Flames can navigate the connection in the direction of their choosing. They can be mindful of this energetic dance and use it to supercharge their healing and development to reach a state of harmonious balance.

But until both individuals are healed and reach a state of acceptance and surrender, the energy will be polarized in one way or another.

Chapter 2

The Runner-Chaser Stage

In the early days with my Twin Flame, it was like the universe was cosmically designed for us to explore. The world was our oyster. Managing such high energy in a relationship can be challenging for the most seasoned spiritual gurus and energy workers. As two young adults who didn't even know what we were experiencing exactly, we didn't have the emotional maturity needed to exert healthy boundaries. We couldn't handle the intensity of our connection with prudence and grace.

After the exhilarating highs of a blissful, ecstatic period, the energy polarized in the other direction. We'd get caught up in petty things. We'd argue and bicker, sometimes about nothing at all. The intense passion we possessed for one another triggered our pride. It was a contrived response. We should've translated our love into selfless acts, service, and gentleness. But our young age and lack of life experience resulted in pride and ego. It aroused doubt and fear—the ingredients for dysfunction.

All the while this was brewing, we remained entranced by how amazingly unreal our love was. We couldn't understand *why* it was so powerful and different. Instead of trying to explore it, we let ourselves get lost in the idea of one another and detach from the real world to dream of our future together. We fantasized about what our house would look like and came up with baby names for our future children.

The option to take this path together in life was laid out for us like a divine gift from the universe. Having this clarity was also scary. It came with a sense of responsibility and realness we couldn't hide from. Add the intensity of a Twin Flame bond on top of that, and you're looking at a tough road ahead.

It triggered the infamous runner-chaser stage—a very common part of the Twin Flame journey, where one person distances themselves from the connection, which prompts the other to chase them and get them back (think back to the note on *The Dance of Twin Flame Energy*).

Trouble in Paradise

I was a petite, blond, college-aged girl living 120 miles away for undergrad. Because of the distance, he had no way of knowing what I was doing during the week. The stereotype of wild parties, experimentation, and casual encounters at university haunted Greg.

Greg struggled to trust my word. This created tension between us and caused endless arguing. I didn't understand why my truth was being questioned in the first place. I didn't know that it was coming from a place of inner fear. I live my life with a personal responsibility to address my shortcomings and issues—whether by healing, fixing, or managing them—to avoid any negative influence on my behavior or hurting other people. "Hurt people, hurt people," as they say. I assumed that Greg shared this perspective, but I underestimated the power of doubt, fear, and insecurity.

Trauma and Healing

Many Twin Flames have experienced trauma or abuse, including sexual and emotional abuse. For some, it creates a trauma bond. But the partners are meant to come together and surface these unresolved pieces so they can be healed and made whole. Through their healing, Twin Flames are meant to rediscover what intimacy means.

The definition of "intimacy" the world uses is flawed, but the Twin Flame journey redefines intimacy. It shows us intimacy on levels that are indescribable—impossible to put into words because it's such a surreal, sacred paradigm of love that we experience. It permeates one's very soul! This level of love is what we're here to activate in the world.

Three months into my time away at undergrad, the struggles of a long-distance relationship began to eat away at Greg. He'd left his heart so open that the unresolved trauma caused by disloyalty and infidelity in past relationships pierced right through it. Doubtful thoughts became twisted and skewed until they were totally transformed into something unrecognizable. This nasty cloud of dismay accumulated and got bigger and bigger, distorting everything it touched within its thick haze.

Instead of releasing thoughts of doubt like, "I wonder if she really went to study hall or if she's at that party she mentioned earlier," Greg held onto them. He didn't realize that by doing so, he was feeding them.

What you focus on grows, and he was focusing on his doubts. This triggered deeper pain and memories of having been lied to or deceived in previous relationships to the point where he couldn't see where his past pain ended and our relationship began.

The Trap of Past Relationships and Expectations

Any time you apply old ways of thinking or old beliefs to a new situation, it'll end poorly. The more you think about what *could* go wrong, the more space you create for that problem to occur. You increase the possibility of it and bring it into existence by holding it so close to you. Doubtful thoughts must be released. It's normal for us to have these thoughts, but it becomes unhealthy when we allow them to rule our situation. "Let go or be dragged," as they say.

Love is the constant in a relationship—a totem of faith that's unquestionable and universal. When times get tough, if a person doesn't keep their sights focused on love, there's room for doubt to grow. This doubt festers and contaminates everything that a person perceives. It brings their deepest fears and "what-ifs" to life. If they consider the idea that their loved one *could* hurt them, then they feed into that possibility and are unintentionally co-creating it into reality.

Fear is why people are so reactive, defensive, or all-around difficult to interact with. It can cause someone to project that fear onto their partner, as if *they* were the one doing wrong. If this goes on for too long, they'll lose sight of the fact that this originated from within themselves and begin to blame it on the outside world: their spouse, their family, their job. None of these things can solve the problems they're trying to fix because the issues are *internal* within them and not "out there."

Greg was having trouble curbing his doubt. This was a big red flag that something was up. His behavior and unwarranted paranoia about my loyalty signaled that he hadn't healed from his past experiences. He carried these things with him in true "wounded warrior" fashion. But by not properly healing them, they seeped into his perceptions and infected his view of our relationship.

Wanting the pain to stop, Greg looked beyond himself to provide relief from his problems when really, they were symptoms of his inner issues—things that needed to be resolved within his own self. This led to him doing something I never thought he'd do.

It's hard to believe that someone who loves their mate so intensely and is tied to them at their very soul could engage in acts of vicious betrayal. But that's exactly what happened when Greg's fear went unchecked.

The Betrayal (Greg's Folly)

Aside from the trust issues that the long distance of our relationship caused, my pursuit of a college education acted as a mirror for Greg. Seeing me go to school prompted him to think about his future. He made the choice to enroll in a local community college. I was happy he was interested in growing and developing. Little did I know this innocent decision would lead to *not* such innocent events. This is how Greg met *her*.

Greg met Jen in a class they had together. Jen was around our age and lived in an apartment she shared with her boyfriend. (Yes, she had a boyfriend, just as Greg had a girlfriend.) Jen was dissatisfied with her relationship, and since Greg perceived the fear he projected onto our relationship as reality, he echoed her sentiment. They bonded over this and found solace from their struggles in one another—a good old-fashioned trauma bond. They secretly dated for months before I caught wind of their closeted affair.

I admit, it took longer than it should've for me to wise up to his infidelity. It was Greg's choice of partner that ultimately gave it away. Humans are very reflective in the sense that we absorb the behaviors and personalities of the people we're exposed to and reflect those onto the things we do, think, and feel. The people we surround ourselves with affect our internal state and social nuances to where changes can be detected by others around us.

Jen was a very angry and vulgar person (and I'm not just saying that because she was my boyfriend's secret lover). Neither Greg nor I were naturally quick to anger. Anger is like kryptonite to me—it's not in my normal array of emotions, and it's very abrasive when I see it expressed in other people. So, when bouts of anger became visible in Greg's behavior, it was clear something was wrong.

This led me to suspicion, but the straw that finally broke the camel's back was the physical evidence I found on Greg's laptop.

Caught Red-Handed

Greg was acting particularly ornery one day, and I'd had enough. I didn't understand why he was treating me in such a nasty way. He was at work, and I was alone in his room. His laptop was open on the coffee table. I couldn't help but take a peek.

Clicking through his collection of images, I noticed a separate file folder. It only had one photo in it. I clicked to open it and saw a picture taken from the laptop's webcam of a blond-haired girl leaning in from behind to give him a kiss. The lighting was poor, and it was heavily pixelated. But I was blond, so I initially figured it was me. There was just one problem: I didn't remember taking that picture.

This was around 2009, back when webcam quality wasn't all that great. The average camera ranged from one to three megapixels. Compare that to the 200-megapixels that the leading Android smartphone in 2023 offers, and you can see how it'd be tough to differentiate one blond girl from another with *one* megapixel quality.

You can imagine the mixed bag of emotions I felt when I realized it wasn't me in the photo. It was Jen. Time seemed to stop, but this time not in a good way. I felt all the blood rush to my gut and a surge of shock and adrenaline. My mind struggled to accept what my eyes were seeing because it didn't make logical sense for someone who loved me so much to engage in such an act.

Into the Mirror

Twin Flames are always connected energetically. Many times, people aren't conscious of the energetic influence coming from their partner because it's not detected with "normal" senses. It's recognized after the fact, in retrospect.

The two partners constantly affect one another at the subtle levels. They send and receive signals that get inferred through their chakra systems, energy fields, and higher selves. By the time a partner's energy manifests into the other's reality, it can appear in a way that is entirely different from how it originally came in. This is because of the distortion from the ego, which applies belief systems and personal perceptions that morph it into something else.

Greg and I were no different. The energetic effects of Greg's battle with his ego and all of his unresolved doubt, insecurity, and fear were reflected onto me. This mirroring effect added another layer of complication. His energy intertwined with my own to where I couldn't tell what was mine and what was his.

While Greg was seeing Jen, he formed toxic traits. He'd turn things around on me, as if it was something that *I* was doing that was destroying the relationship. He was so reactive to everything I did or said. These painful encounters were the effect of Greg's irrational attempt to resolve his guilt and shame. The pain from these instances slowly dimmed my light.

I started to reflect this low-vibrational, low-level energy in my own thoughts, feelings, and behaviors. It manifested in the form of jealousy, distrust, and anger. I couldn't understand what was making me act this way. Where was all this coming from? Lo and behold, it was the energetic effect of being so deeply connected to my Twin Flame.

The heartbreak of Greg's betrayal triggered my most intense dive into the darkness to date. I'd endured some very dark, nasty things in early childhood (think abuse). But the depression that hit after learning that Greg was involved with another woman was the darkest I'd ever experienced. My entire world was torn into pieces. I'd opened my heart, only for him to consciously choose to see someone else and betray my trust.

TL;DR

Uncovering Greg's secret relationship tore me apart. Things with him became painfully rocky. Over the next four years, we tried to make it work, but our wounds just wouldn't heal. It brought on four years of an on-again, off-again back-and-forth between us.

At this time in my life, I became what Greg called, "spiteful." Damn right, I was! I'd been loyal to him despite the distance between us or his paranoid accusations that I was doing *him* wrong. I did everything I could to be a good partner, only to find that it wasn't enough. I recalled all the times he hung up quickly when we talked on the phone or the delay in his text message replies. Was he with her then? How could I have been so blind?!

The Runner-Chaser, Amtrak Edition

There's much more I could share about this era of turbulence, like the time I chased a train from Charlotte to Cary, North Carolina, out of heartache and frustration.

Traveling by train was easier and cheaper than driving for Greg to come to see me at school. We'd finished up a weekend visit that wasn't too great. There was so much tension between us and tons of pain from the aftermath of his betrayal. We were arguing when he boarded the train to go home. He stopped answering my texts and wouldn't pick up my calls.

I insisted on being heard. I followed the train in my little 1998 Toyota Camry, jamming out to emotional songs about heartache and romantic injustice. I stopped at every stop the train did on the one-in-a-million chance he'd see me. I wanted him to *know* how much he was affecting me. See my pain. And make it better, somehow.

Looking back, it was highly unlikely he'd see me from the train. But my actions were ruled by immediacy and not reason.

When he got off at his stop in Cary, he was surprised to see me. I'm sure you can figure that it didn't go well from there.

This literal rendition of Twin Flame runner-chaser energy did exactly what you'd think it would... it made the chaser (me) chase harder and the runner (him) run faster.

Choosing the 3 Fs of Love

Eventually, I made the choice to love myself by no longer subjecting myself to his behavior. I left the chase of the Twin Flame dynamic entirely. True love means *self*-love. And staying in something like that isn't treating yourself with the utmost self-respect and love.

Learning to love yourself and guard your heart is an essential part of an awakening, and it was necessary for me to gain an intimate understanding of forgiveness. Forgiveness can only be granted when you've fully accepted things for what they are. You've healed whatever it is within yourself that's kept you from moving forward. If any part of you is holding on to things that no longer serve you, including doubt or the fear of being hurt again, you can't embody the **3 Fs of love: freely, fearlessly,** and **fully.**

I grew to accept the unfortunate fact that I had to go through that. The infidelity, the betrayal, the mirroring... all of it. Like a broken bone that heals stronger than it was before, I had to break my heart so I could put it back together again—this time with the right foundation.

Chapter 3

The Separation Stage

I finished college and moved back home to start an internship at a Fortune 500 company. At the ripe age of twenty-two, I had my whole life ahead of me. Though I was now living in the same city as Greg, I couldn't pursue a life with him. He had more growing to do—more things to realize in himself before he could handle our relationship with the integrity and care it deserved.

I completely cut Greg out of my life so that I could move forward. I blocked his phone number and social media profiles. I acted as if he didn't exist. I hate to say it, but as if he was *dead to me*.

This period of separation lasted for seven years. I turned my focus on milestones like getting married, buying a house, and building a family and a fruitful career. All the material success in the world couldn't fill the spiritual, metaphysical hole in my soul. Greg also struggled to feel whole. He prayed that he'd one day have another chance at being with me.

Separation Stage of Twin Flames

Twin Flame couples go through what's called the separation stage—a period where they aren't together. During this time, they appear to drift apart and may even date other people. But they always remain connected at higher levels.

It can be a painful time of yearning and heartache, but it's a very important one. It's needed for the partners to gain objectivity. It gives a much-needed pause in the relationship to allow time to process, integrate, and grow in ways like shedding false beliefs of what we're taught a "good" relationship should be.

For instance, some people might think that if they're in a serious relationship, they must always be near their partner; otherwise, it means something's wrong. This belief can become skewed, and they perceive distance from their partner as punishment. How unhealthy and untrue is that? We're *always* connected to our loved one!

The separation stage creates space to dispel self-conceived notions like these that keep people from being in harmonic union. We learn not to hold others to the personal standards or expectations of how we *think* they should be. We learn to accept that things are happening as they should, as the universe requires—not as we demand them to be.

Making the Switch from Twin Flame to Soulmate

With the possibility of a future with Greg struck down, it was time for me to move on. I wasn't consciously searching for someone new but didn't realize the energy I was putting out into the universe was speaking for me. That's when a soulmate, Mike, came into the picture.

Mike had recently moved back into town after trying his luck in California. He'd gotten out of an intense relationship with his ex-girlfriend and wasn't necessarily looking for love yet, either. We knew each other from a party back in high school. We kept each other in our peripheral view over the years, occasionally glancing at social media to see what the other was up to. But the timing was never right for us to make a connection. Now, our paths were fated to cross.

Too many things seemed like divine timing, and I took this as a green light from the universe to pursue my connection with Mike. From our very first date, we hit it off. We were practically inseparable after that. There were some growing pains a couple of months into dating, which I saw as natural effects of us realizing that the relationship could actually go somewhere. It was "marriage material." The patterns, trends, and things from our pasts were surfacing to be healed and make room for something new.

Mike was a Capricorn and grounded in the material world. I craved this stability. He showed every sign of being a soulmate. A long-term commitment with a soulmate isn't as chaotic as it is with a Twin Flame. A soulmate enters your life to fulfill a purpose or complete a chapter in your life, whereas a Twin Flame is a connection over multiple lifetimes designed to facilitate your overarching spiritual development.

Choosing a Path

The promise of consistency with Mike was a breath of fresh air. After the turbulent, dramatic rollercoaster of a relationship with Greg, the stable relationship with Mike was a godsend. It was like the most glorious drink of water after years of being stranded in the desert. I could see the water glistening in the oasis ahead that would finally quench my thirst.

Mike entered my life like the universe divinely called him to offer me relief. The path with Mike was different and led to a calm, contained lake of water. With Greg, it was like a fast-flowing river with choppy white-water rapids that led to a gigantic waterfall. While what Mike offered wasn't as powerful as the waterfall, it was what I needed at the time.

There weren't as many obstacles involved, either. A waterfall has a rapidly moving river that's nice to float atop, but the current can quickly sweep you under. To make it down to the bliss-like, serene pool of water below, you'd have to ride the fast-moving water and cascade down with it at each stage of the fall. The pool of water it leads to is a greater reward than the still lake the other path offers. The flowing waterfall is endlessly supplying it. But the journey to get there is tumultuous. Some people would say it isn't worth the risk or the struggle and would choose the predictable surety of the lake. I made my decision to pursue the latter.

By this point, Greg was still attempting to reach me by snail mail. Mike and I had been taking photos together, being an excited new couple and all. When the next letter came from Greg, I crafted a coldhearted reply and enclosed a picture of Mike and me. It was reminiscent of how I found out about his secret lover, Jen, with a photo.

This cruel, vengeful method worked. Greg stopped pursuing me. I was free to explore my relationship with Mike, whom I married in 2015 and started a life with. However, the shockwaves from my chosen method to separate from Greg would be felt for years to come.

The Fulfillment You Desire Comes from Within

The power of Twin Flame partners gets amplified when they come together. The two people's energies merge to create something greater than the sum of its parts. If one or both of the Twins fail to "clear the mirror" or heal themselves, it causes an up-and-down, rollercoaster relationship until those lessons are realized and actualized.

This means your individual sense of self is critical for your relationship's dynamic. Both you and your partner must realize that internal healing cannot come from external sources: the love and assurance you desire come from within.

Seeking a relationship to fill the void you have inside conflicts with the higher lesson of universal love. Relying on your Twin Flame (or anyone else, for that matter) to make you feel the love and wholeness you should feel yourself does two things:

1. It places unwarranted responsibility on the other person, making them accountable for something that only you can

provide. This sets unattainable standards for your partner and creates a sense of lack in your perception of them.

2. It limits and restricts the other person to fitting into *your* expectations of how they should be. You're not giving them room to shine in their full potential or love you in their own way. It's the opposite of allowing them to be free. And that's not love.

Looking to your Twin Flame for inner fulfillment is something that's founded in fear—the fear of what would happen if you had to look *internally* for fulfillment, if you had to face yourself and dive into the depths of your soul to become comfortable with yourself, and if you released the expectations of how your Twin Flame relationship should unfold. It's a fear-driven attempt to control the relationship rather than letting it flourish and thrive organically. Trying to control anything other than your own self never turns out well.

The Twin Flame journey teaches the importance of knowing that you are whole and complete just the way you are. "Home" is found within you, not within your partner.

Chapter 4

2012: The End Is ~~Near~~ Cycling

I can't help but notice that the separation from my Twin Flame occurred in 2012. People thought the world would end in 2012 because the last cycle of the Mesoamerican Long Count calendar was marked on December 12, 2012, also known as the "zero date." It was such a big deal that major news outlets covered it, big Hollywood movies were produced, and the airwaves lit up with the world's chatter about whether we'd see our doom.

The significance of 2012 is that it is the end of a 5,126-year cycle in the Mesoamerican Long Count calendar. This calendar was used by the Maya, Aztecs, and other Mesoamerican cultures to track time. The end of this cycle was seen by some as a sign of the end of the world. The Maya themselves did not believe that the world would end in 2012. They simply saw it as the beginning of a new cycle.

I won't go into a deep analysis of what this calendar really meant, as obviously, the world didn't end in 2012, but there are a few important themes to make a note of:

Time. The Mayan view of time is different from ours. They saw time from a nonlinear perspective and viewed things through a lens of cycles and connections of the past, present, and future. You might think, "But wait … that sounds *exactly* like how we see time." Developments in quantum physics and other fields of study have put us on a trajectory to understand time in a similar way that the Maya understood it. But that's a very recent belief that's still reaching mainstream culture.

Spirituality. The Maya interwove spirituality into their culture, including daily practices and social norms. Today, the world is making its pilgrimage back to merging spiritual beliefs with our view of the world. Humanity is cycling back to this way of being.

Cycles. The Mayan Long Count calendar maps out cycles or baktuns of 144,000 days. The number 144,000 holds significance in the spiritual community, from Christians and Mormons to Starseeds and pseudospiritualists. Additionally, the final cycle of the calendar ended on December 21, 2012. The meanings of numerology of the number 1 (new beginnings and the start of a new cycle) and the number 2 (duality and balance), as well as the divinity of the number 12, can all be noticed in this date.

It's important to note the similarities across cultures, religions, and eras. They're indicative of our connected universe. These points of connection aren't just apparent in your individual life, like seeing 11:11 p.m. on the clock. These are life's *embeddings*, prevailing throughout human history, current events, and anything organic to provide the deeper meaning of something greater.

Connected Through Space and Time

Even after cutting ties with Greg and marrying Mike, the connection with my Twin Flame remained. Greg's magnetic pull could break through anything I was feeling or doing at the time and reach me with ease through metaphysical channels. I could feel the call of his energy—intense moments of thought or emotion when he called me into his heart. The telepathy and empathy between us overwhelmed me and interrupted my day-to-day life.

It was like he was purposely thinking about me and using our connection to get my attention. Like he had an energetic telephone and was calling me, hoping to trigger a response (or playfully annoy me, at least). When he called, I'd hear it "ring" on my end. When I wouldn't pick up the phone to invite his energy in, it still affected me at the deepest levels.

I felt guilty. I was married to Mike but stuck in the throes of Greg's connection. I felt frustrated that after all my attempts to disconnect, I couldn't escape our magnetism.

Forever Connected: The Silver Cord

Twin Flames are categorized by the profound, inseverable connection that ties them together. This is the silver cord, also known as the astral cord. The silver cord tethers one Twin Flame to the other and can be used for metaphysical communication. It's like a direct uplink to their counterpart.

This is how Twin Flames stay connected during the separation stage, or when one Twin Flame leaves Earth (dies) and goes back to Spirit. It's what kept my connection with Greg open.

The Silver Cord

The silver cord is the metaphysical link that connects your higher self to your physical body at the solar plexus chakra (this is where the phrase "solar plexus pull" comes from). It also allows energy to pass through the heart space.

It's tethered to your higher self in the spiritual plane, connecting from your physical body through each of your subtle bodies; hence, its other name, the *astral cord*. The cord itself goes much farther than the astral plane and reaches all the way into higher dimensions and planes.

Evidence of this intangible, unbreakable cord can be found in areas like astrology and religion. The constellation of Pisces features a cord that connects the two fish, with each fish representing one of the dualistic sides of life (material and spiritual). In the Bible, the silver cord is mentioned as being critical for life to flow through.

"Remember your Creator now while you are young, before the silver cord of life snaps and the golden bowl is broken... For then

While cord-cutting is a helpful practice to break bonds with people at the soul level, cord-cutting won't work with your Twin Flame. Since Twin Flames share the same silver cord, your Twin's cord is your cord. And you cannot cut your own cord. However, you can still distance yourself from the connection if you so choose. Practices like clearing the mirror and energy healing are often used by Twin Flames to accomplish this.

The Entanglement of Addiction and Health

I can't tell this story without mentioning the opioid epidemic. Back in the 2010s, people abused opioids in the form of legal pharmaceuticals. Greg and I were no exception. Fentanyl patches were our "drugs of choice." He was able to hold a job while using, and I graduated college, worked full-time, and exceled in meeting society's expectations of normalcy. The use carried over into my relationship with Mike, who had his own substance abuse issues. Both relationships were subject to issues that are typical of addicts, like prioritizing drugs over your partner.

The addicted mind is always subconsciously focused on the next hit. This takes up valuable cognitive resources to be fully open or in the moment with your loved one. In tarot, it's referred to as a "third-party relationship," where the substance is the third party. A thing can be just as hazardous to a relationship as a person (like a secret lover) if it becomes something they idolize.

As I worked the recovery journey, it became impossible to ignore how much substances, including legally prescribed medications, numbed the subtle body. A substance doesn't alleviate things; it masks them. It acts like a thick fog that limits one's receptors both physically and metaphysically. Once I got off substances, I noticed my intuition was sharper. My emotional depth returned. The fine-tuning of my body readjusted.

The takeaway is undeniable: The medicines we put in our bodies (legal or otherwise) influence our energetic templates and alter the effectiveness of our nonphysical senses. Their effects create a veil that reduces our sensory perception in ways that can be difficult to detect. This was even more reason for me to continue pursuing my recovery, which led to spiritual awakening.

The spiritual awakening was calling all parts of me into alignment with my expanding view of spirituality, including the body. The body gives us multiple similarities, hints, and clues to better understand the dynamics of our physical being and the energies it can experience.

Duality

Your body is a stark example of the principle of duality. Like the yin and yang, your body has two "brains," the mind and the gut. Your gut has over 100 million *neurons* (yes, neurons) from your esophagus to your rectum. So, neurons aren't only in the brain.

Like the yin and yang, the mind and gut systematically regulate the central nervous system and the enteric nervous system. The food you eat not only affects the health of your gut, but it also affects your ability to physically create. I'm talking about your cells.

Every day, 1% of your body's regeneratable cells are replaced (1% is approximately 330 billion cells). In about three months, 100% of the 30 trillion cell population that makes up "you" will be regenerated. Your body uses the food you eat to do this.

If you already knew your body has a second brain and regenerates its cells, did you know there's a literal light inside you? OK, not literally, but you do have something called the *lumen*, which is fascinating. It's located in your gastrointestinal system and is the opening inside of your bowels. Its name resembles the Latin word, lūmen, which means "light." When you think about how your body digests food to regenerate cells, like your skin, it brings a whole new meaning to the phrase, "You're glowing!"

The gut also contains the celiac plexus, also known as the solar plexus, which is a major collection of nerves near the aorta and diaphragm. In the chakra system, the chakra at the upper abdominal area is called the solar plexus. I could go on and on about the connections in the body, mind, and spirit, like these.

The more I learned about the significance of the gut in both physical and spiritual respects, the more I found myself gravitating away from certain foods, foods that were heavily processed or meats like chicken and low-quality cuts of beef. My appetite shifted to desire high-vibrational, alkaloid foods like kale, lime, and almonds—even before I knew that they were. Food gets processed to balance the body's pH level. The more acidic the pH level is, the more health problems and diseases (or "*dis*-eases") a person will have.

The body is the gateway to metaphysical connection. Herein lies the need to keep it in balance.

Everything in *balance*.

Chapter 5

The Near-Death Experience

Three years before the separation cycle from Greg would end, I had a brush with death that resulted in an unusual near-death experience (NDE). It was a critical step toward expanding my perception of the universe and what's possible.

After the birth of my daughter in 2016, I suffered postpartum complications from an undetected uterine bleed. To paint a picture of my critical condition, here's an excerpt of my medical rap sheet before I was intubated (aka put on life support):

- C-section
- Liver failure
- E. coli infection
- Kidney failure
- Sepsis
- Dual uterine artery embolization
- Exploratory surgery
- Uterine bleed
- Dialysis
- Blood transfusions
- Fluid in lungs and stomach
- Acute respiratory Distress Syndrome
- DVT blood clots

My husband went against the advice of my doctors and life-flighted me to another hospital. It just so happened that my husband's aunt worked as an OR nurse in the exact department I needed to be transferred into, so I ended up at the University of Virginia at Charlottesville (UVA) Hospital. This was despite having three nationally acclaimed hospitals within 30 minutes of my hometown. Another remarkable coincidence of landing at this hospital is that UVA's Division of Perceptual Studies is known for its research of perceptual phenomena like NDEs.

My family was told to say their goodbyes, and I was intubated and placed in a medically induced coma to slow the damage and make my death more comfortable. While unconscious, my dreams were wildly vivid. This is interesting when you consider that a medically induced coma is designed to reduce brain activity almost to a standstill.

My body approached the "near-death" threshold, and my consciousness left my body. That's when my dreams went from playing out figments of my subconscious to something more like a glitch in the matrix. Things get a little fuzzy here, but the next thing I clearly recall was my soul's will to live.

The Death Track

The original hospital I was at instilled a ton of fear. While I was under, I heard everything the nurses, doctors, and medical staff said. And it wasn't pretty. I was convinced they were trying to kill me. That may be a strong statement, but they certainly weren't trying to keep me alive. This was nerve-wracking.

Add to that, when I woke up to see the familiar faces of my friends and family, I instinctively detected that they were somehow different from who they were in my present reality. It was a very alienating and, in some moments, unsafe feeling, like I didn't belong. I needed to find a way back to my time.

At one point, I encountered a malicious presence that encouraged me to die. A light appeared in the dark void. The disembodied voice tried to convince me to "let go."

"Everyone will understand," it said, referring to my loved ones. "It would be OK if you chose to let go."

I dubbed this voice the "death track" because it kept playing like a track on repeat, urging me to make the choice to die. It scared me because I did not know who or what was trying to lure me in. It didn't feel like the devil (but then again, would it if it really was him?). Or perhaps it was a normal, benevolent entity, and the idea of dying is what had me so spooked.

In this nonphysical realm of darkness, I maneuvered away from the light (best understood as "the light at the end of the tunnel") using my intention and will. Since I wasn't in my body at this point, my consciousness was not operating with the normal logic that our brains use. My thoughts were happening at the *soul level*. It was similar to a fight-or-flight, life-or-death response, but my goal was not to survive as a human. It was to protect my soul. My soul was on a mission to live out this life and fulfill the purpose I was born for. I made my choice accordingly and set the intention to live.

My Existence In The Beyond

While unconscious, I existed in a place beyond the 3D material realm and was on a mission to return to my body. Something odd took place in all of this; when my soul tried to find the right point in reality to tie itself back to, I got stuck in a loop of reliving the same day over and over ... each time playing out with a different set of circumstances—a different possibility in the quantum field. My friends and family, the lunch I ate, the demeanor of the medical staff, and the hospital environment around me were slightly different each time. But the date was always the same: August 27, 2016.

Some might call these differences alternate universes or timelines, but the experience doesn't quite match those definitions. This was a journey through the fabric of the quantum field—navigating through the network of infinite possibilities to land on the one that fit my newly calibrated life path.

Slipping Into Groundhog Day

I awoke from my medically induced coma on August 27, 2016. I was in the ICU, bedridden and hooked up to a ton of machinery that had been keeping me alive. My vision was blurred from the gel that was used to moisten my eyes while incubated, but I was able to make out the large handwriting on the whiteboard. It had my doctor's name and date written on it.

My husband was sitting by my bedside. He was surprised and happy to see me come to. He tried to explain that I had been transferred to another hospital, but I was too out of it to understand. My body was exhausted from the intense medical battle it was fighting. I was just happy to know I'd survived, and with that, I drifted off to sleep.

I woke up the next morning and remembered that I'd come to the day before. I remembered waking up from my coma and talking with my husband. The nurse asked me if I knew where I was, who the president was, and today's date—the typical questions for ICU patients. I got two out of three right.

For the date, I responded, "It's August 28."

The nurse quickly corrected me, "No, it's August 27."

I didn't know what to make of this. I figured it might be a case of residual medical delirium from the heavy anesthesia still in my system. Eventually, my body grew tired, and I fell asleep again.

The third time I woke up, again on August 27, it was clear that this was not delirium or confusion.

Every time I came to, I instinctively detected that something was amiss. It wasn't the reality I was supposed to be in. There were differences in people's personalities, the way they behaved, and the events that unfolded. I experienced this cycle of waking up on the same day but in a different iteration or reality at least a dozen times.

Experiencing Other Timelines

In one timeline, I might've been awake for a couple of days by that point because I was able to eat lunch (when a patient wakes from being in a coma for so long, they have to be cleared to eat solid food safely). Soon after finishing my meal, I began to vomit violently. The ICU staff rushed in and surrounded me in a panic.

The lunch I'd eaten earlier was coming up, and I recognized it not from that day but from an "earlier" timeline I had lived in before. (I put "earlier" in quotes because it was like I was experiencing these multiple timelines all at once, so it's hard to tell what came before or after. Not every timeline was different enough to disseminate as distinct or unique, so it's possible that I experienced more timelines than I remember.)

The doctor arrived and broke through the circle of ICU attendants to examine me. Then, they performed an emergency procedure to intubate me again while I was still conscious. I was unable to speak during this scene of chaos, but my husband saw my severe discomfort and said to the medical staff, "Yeah, she doesn't like that," hoping they'd stop.

I passed out after that, exhausted from what had transpired. The experience was traumatizing. But the next time I'd wake up, it would be the morning of August 27, 2016... again.

Trying to Break the Loop

No matter which timeline, reality, or possibility, I always woke up on August 27. From my family's perspective, I was waking up for the first time. From my perspective, I'd already lived this moment multiple times. I knew the first words my husband would say to me when he looked over and saw I was awake. I'd memorized them from the realities I'd heard them in before.

I was so tired of living the same sequence: my family's response, my husband being so excited to show me pictures of my daughter, who I hadn't even gotten to really hold yet, and then waiting until I fell asleep again for it to start all over again and try to escape the loop. After so many go-arounds of this, I grew impatient and frustrated by being stuck in this loop.

I knew the chain of events that played out upon waking from my coma, so I had the opportunity to try saying different things to see if it would change the sequence of events. I tried to think of ways that I could get my husband's attention and explain what was happening to me.

The next time I awoke, my husband welcomed me with his repeated greeting of, "Hey, beautiful." Right on cue. My response was rushed.

"We've already had this conversation," I said, hoping that this would alert him to what I was experiencing.

In another instance, when I woke up, I tried to say his words, "Hey, beautiful," before he did to prove that I'd already experienced it and knew what would happen next. I expected him to say something like, "Wow, how did you know I would say that?" But starting the conversation myself instead of waiting for him to speak first changed the outcome of that reality, so his words were not the same.

Defeated, I realized it was impossible to alert Mike to what was going on. He wasn't in the same loop. This was an isolating, distant feeling. There was no hope for other people to know what I was experiencing. I was all alone in this, wading through the fabric of space and time. While I had knowledge of the other timelines, the people around me weren't part of the loop. They existed in the vacuum of their singular reality. I couldn't reach them or get them to understand.

It made me question if the iterations of my family members in these timelines were conscious—were their souls present and remembering our interactions? Or was I witnessing some type of quantum projection of them, like a holographic shell with no soul or consciousness tied to it? This made me feel even more alone. I had to get back to the iteration of reality that intersected all our souls.

Entering a New Body

The feeling when I entered a "new" body in each timeline is something I'll never forget. It was a familiar feeling, like I'd experienced it before. But what wasn't familiar was the sense that when I entered this "new" body, something was off. (It was always *my* body but in a different iteration of reality, so the body was technically "new" compared to what my soul was used to.)

My soul knew I wasn't where I should be. I felt like an alien in a foreign place. It was familiar enough to look like home, but everything about it felt off. I innately knew my soul was calibrated specifically for a different version of reality. It's like standing in a room with ninety-nine other people who are wearing red while you're wearing purple. You're human like they are. You're wearing clothes like they are. You're even standing like they are. But there's one subtle difference: the color of your clothing. You see everyone else in red outfits and become utterly aware that you don't fit in with your purple attire. In other words, you don't belong. That is how it felt to wake up in a timeline that didn't quite fit my etheric template.

The loop of waking up on the same day over and over again was beginning to take a toll. I didn't know when this never-ending cycle would end. I couldn't trust the forward flow of time. Knowing that I'd have to relive this loop made going to sleep terrifying. Every time I woke up on August 27, I'd have to wait anywhere from four to twenty-four hours to fall back to sleep for the "reset" to occur. By the time I landed in this current reality, I was spiritually and physically exhausted.

A Displaced Soul Fragment Drifting Through the Quantum Field

Through all of this, I never questioned my sanity. I somehow knew that what I was witnessing went beyond my physical body. It wasn't a matter of my mental state. Whatever was going on dealt with a much higher level. My soul was attempting to find its way back to reality's right point of possibility.

Perhaps my soul was displaced from having almost died. Maybe it detached from my body to visit my soul family in the nonphysical realm that so many NDE survivors tell of. When I made the choice to live, maybe its wires got crossed to find its way back through the quantum field. If my soul detected that the version or point of possibility wasn't the right fit, maybe the process repeated until I found the correct one, and that caused the Groundhog Day time loop effect.

My soul was jumping through the quantum field, hopping along the points of possibility to find the right fit. The NDE reconfigured my body, mind, and spirit. I was jumping to different iterations of reality to find the one that aligned with my new existence.

The closer I got to my intended timeline, the smoother the jumps were and the calmer I felt. Time began to behave normally again, too, and I finally made it to the next day, August 28th!

This was short-lived. My body was still in intensive recovery, so I never stayed awake for long. I fell back to sleep and landed on the 27th again. But it was a huge milestone. Reaching the 28th meant I was getting closer to exiting the loop. And I finally did.

The Power to Heal

When I awoke from my coma, I was completely immobile. Due to the extreme swelling, the wound from multiple surgeries, the loss of muscle mass from being in stasis, and all the medical trauma, I couldn't walk. I couldn't even stand up without assistance. It took one week for me to be able to sit up and scootch to the edge of the bed, step down into a walker, and then shuffle over to the ICU room sink a few feet away to wash my hands.

The doctors' best-case scenario was for a six-month recovery, beginning with three months in an inpatient rehab facility to regain mobility. I had to learn how to walk all over again. Also, my surgical wound would require special care. As a first-time mother with a newborn to tend to, the thought that I'd miss the first six months of my daughter's life and not get to care for her was devastating.

To everyone's surprise, my health did a complete 180 as soon as I transferred out of the ICU and onto the general floor. I began healing at an unexplainable rate. By the fourth day, I was taking short steps from my hospital bed to the door of my room with the help of a rolling walker. The plans for physical therapy or rehab after my release vanished into the ether. They weren't needed. I was healing at the same rate as, if not faster than, the descent toward my NDE had taken.

Many people who've been on the verge of death live to explain how they miraculously survived stage four cancer or how they lived for years after doctors told them they were in their final days. The study of how one's mental-emotional state signals the body to overcome disease or heal chronic ailments is gaining esteem in the scientific community, and my story is no different.

The doctors, residents, and hospital staff had no explanation for my miraculous recovery. It was something empowered by the Spirit side of the universe, something that can't be fully explained by medical science alone.

Chapter 6

The Setup for a Tragic Ending... and Rebirth

The NDE was traumatizing but eye-opening. This was around the time the Berenstein Bears vs. Berenstain Bears controversy was going on. The multiverse theory was gaining popularity. I talked with a coworker about my experience, and her response was something I hadn't heard of before. She said my NDE sounded like the Mandela Effect. The way she described the Mandela Effect was eerily similar to what I had witnessed.

Consider our reality as a bubble that's constantly in motion. There are other bubbles (realities) bunched up around it. Those touching the main bubble's boundaries are the most similar to it. The ones farther out are different. The farther out you go, the more unrecognizable they become from the main bubble. Being in motion, they're constantly bumping into, merging with, and breaking off from one another. After the way I experienced my NDE, this rang a bell with me. If that's the nature of reality, then it makes sense that my soul might've had trouble pinpointing the right spot in space and time to return to.

If my soul or consciousness could experience time and reality in such a different way, then who's to say that the soul itself is not equally as complex as the reality it experiences? When you overlay things like the hierarchy of a soul and the multiple incarnations connected to the higher self with the complexities of time, space, and other dimensions, it points to a world of limitless possibilities.

Life After Near Death

Life went on after the NDE, but my marriage was never the same. The experience took a toll on my husband. The trauma from being told that his wife was going to die, and his newborn baby was in the NICU triggered unhealed trauma from his brother's suicide years earlier.

Mike's casual drinking slowly slipped into alcoholism. I pleaded with him to heal, to take a vacation, to go to rehab... to do *anything* to address these things. His response was always something avoidant, like, "I just need to go to work," as if his job would somehow give him emotional-spiritual fulfillment or resolve his trauma.

This felt like a repeat of my time with Greg when he'd insist that he was working through things within himself as he should, and I'd trust him to do so. Of course, that never happened, and the issues only got more convoluted.

Trying to be a good, supportive wife, I let my husband see to things in his own way. I focused on raising our baby, exceling at my career, and keeping the household running.

At the time, my idea of what classified as the "good life" was influenced by what society says we need to be happy and successful: we must marry, have children, own a home, and so on. I'd learn, however, that one's path doesn't always follow society's rules. In fact, attempting to live by society's standards can fuel feelings of resistance and letdown from trying to live up to someone else's version of happiness.

My life was set up on illusions and unsustainable notions like this. The house of cards soon came tumbling down.

State of Crisis

Life was tearing down and preparing for transformation—truths behind the illusions were being revealed and old ways were crumbling down to make room for something new. It felt like my world was being flipped upside-down. It was a horrible and chaotic feeling.

Things hit a head when my husband unexpectedly left to go to a rehab center in Florida, leaving his two-year-old daughter and me behind.

In the weeks following Mike's departure, I was a wreck. He didn't tell me he was leaving until the day of and gave me no date for his expected return. I didn't know if he'd return at all. I felt abandoned by my spouse (talk about a trauma trigger!).

Every waking moment was spent in fight-or-flight mode, a sheer state of panic to keep all the moving pieces in motion so as not to impact our young daughter's quality of life.

The situation ran me into the ground. My physical and mental health rapidly deteriorated. My body was riddled with anxiety to the point of tremors and shaking hands. Though I was sober then, I appeared worse off than ever.

A quote from the medical records of my NDE came to mind. The statement "I fear she will not be able to survive this" haunted me. Now, it applied to this situation.

The stress of keeping everything afloat grew to be too much to handle alone and unsupported. I had to make a change before I self-destructed. I couldn't keep going at this rate. Something had to give.

Support from the Universe

I accepted that I was alone and afraid. If I wanted anything to change, I'd have to be the one to change it.

With this shift in my attitude came Greg's resurfacing into my world, as if something in the eternal fabric of the universe was triggered and set into motion. Up to that point, we'd been living our lives like two separate galaxy systems, each revolving through space and cycling through the universe, not realizing that a magnetic pull was slowly bringing us back into the other's path. The circumstances were just right for the proverbial stars to align and make it possible for us to come back together.

The end of the separation period from my Twin Flame was accompanied by the closing out of many cycles. I was unprepared and in a state of crisis. I wish I had been more mindful of the shortcomings. I could have steered my life differently with more grace and serenity. By the end of my separation period:

- I was the farthest away I'd ever been from myself. I was so focused on the material side of life that I lost touch with what lights up my soul: the mystical side. Being so consumed with keeping a three-person household running alongside a career, I lacked the time and focus to tap into that side of myself—or even to realize I'd lost touch.
- I lacked faith in God. I didn't trust the process of the universe. I was in chaos and darkness, unable to see the light. Survival mode drove my every intention, thought, and action.
- I didn't have the tools to self-regulate. I had to integrate healthy practices into my life to avoid ever going back to a state of panic when life's abrasive, swift changes would eventually occur again. I never wanted to feel that way again.
- I opted for indolence. I'd just endured a period of tribulations—major life changes, one after the other. I'd had enough turbulence to last me to old age. I longed for calmer skies and went into a period of stasis. I strayed from having to make any decisions that I considered to be "too much," including decisions regarding my Twin Flame relationship. All I wanted was a break to recoup. But life doesn't stop for us to catch our breath. If we don't make a decision for ourselves, one will be made for us.

Divine Timing of Reentry

Greg reentered my life in late June 2019, around the same time of year we'd first started dating back in 2008.

When we broke up in 2012, I genuinely believed I'd never see him again—so much so that my motto about our past relationship was "Never again." Yet, every event since then built on the last, like steppingstones perfectly laid in the direction of reuniting with him.

I didn't yet realize that I *needed* to reunite with Greg to bring my life back into alignment and resolve many of the things left unsaid or that were incomplete between us. We had more work to do together. There was more to learn to activate our greater purpose.

Greg came back into my world like a guardian angel, just in time to stop me from breaking completely. He swooped in like a knight in shining armor to tend to my emotional needs as well as save the day in material ways. He was the perfect person for bringing me back to life and probably the only person who could.

The house I shared with my now-estranged husband, Mike, was aging. It was as old as I was (over three decades) and in need of major repairs. Major expensive repairs. The threat of going into severe debt was imminent if I wasn't proactive.

It was just my luck that Greg worked in his family's general contracting business. Being the kind of person who genuinely wanted to help others and ease their suffering, he got to work and helped me get the house ready for sale. I wouldn't have been able to do it, much less afford it, if not for him.

Greg's presence wasn't the only thing the universe provided me during this catastrophic time. I'd been pursuing a legal settlement from the medical situation (NDE) in 2016. The laws in my state didn't leave me with a great chance of success. But right at the last possible minute in the legal window to file a claim, I got the unexpected news that the party accepted the terms of my settlement.

I'd recently been laid off from my job, unable to maintain consistent performance through everything. The amount I received from the medical claim just happened to equal what my regular salary would have been over the coming months. Another gift from the universe received in divine timing.

The universe always provides. Ask and you shall receive!

The Reunion

Greg's reentry into my life began with casual messages on Facebook (he had a new profile that wasn't blocked). Our conversations were comprised of witty humor and playful banter to cope with the harsh reality of our past pain that lingered beneath the surface. Eventually, we were comfortable enough to see one another, and planned for him to come to my place.

Neither of us knew how it would go. Would it be awkward? Would the spark still be there? Would we find that time got the best of us and deteriorated the connection that once was?

When Greg walked through my front door for the first time in seven years, my first thought was, "Wow, he looks good!" He looked as fit and attractive as he had almost a decade earlier. We got through the awkward hellos but didn't stray far from small talk. We weren't ready to acknowledge the elephant in the room of our shared history.

Greg's authenticity and easy-going nature hadn't changed. It made me want to release all my worries and melt into his presence. He was a smooth talker who could disarm my defenses with only a smile. But Greg was also the only person who, if we were in the same room together, I couldn't resist—the magnetism was too powerful. So I had to keep my guard up.

I distanced myself from him as we talked, careful not to plunge back into the depths of the love we both knew was still there. I was like a recovered alcoholic who goes to a wedding with an open bar. They know danger sits peacefully contained in the bottles nearby, that they're one drink away from derailing their entire world into a relapse, so they make an extra effort to safeguard their sobriety.

At the end of his visit, we embraced in a polite hug, the kind of hug you'd give a typical friend as an expected gesture. We held back on allowing any romantic (or sexual) energy to flow.

As soon as he left my house that night, I felt the energetic floodgates open. The air was electric, and our Twin Flame journey was activated... again. The seven-year separation stage was over, and the next stage was beginning.

Chapter 7

The Runner and the Chaser, Reversed

Now that Greg was back in my life and had time to mature, I couldn't believe he was finally ready for us to be together!

I spent years of our first relationship desperately trying to get Greg to heal his pain so we could be together. Back then, I was the one pushing for growth, change, and development. Now, the tables had turned: Greg was ready to commit to our relationship.

The joke was on me, though, because now *I* wasn't ready. He was the one pushing me to wake up and be my full, true self.

The Fountain of Youth Is Love

When we reunited, I was shocked that Greg looked like he hadn't aged! He still looked like the early twenty-something-year-old I knew before. He was physically fit. His skin was firm and smooth like it was almost a decade earlier. His spirit was not jaded by the world. He had a zest for life and was ready to laugh and enjoy it. Even the look in his eyes was youthful.

Being with Greg was the epitome of feeling "forever young." It made me feel like I was sixteen again. Not just in the sense of getting the anxious, giddy feeling of butterflies in your stomach that you often feel in young love. Greg's love brought a youthful glow to every aspect of my life. My entire being felt "born again." It was exactly what I needed to come back into myself.

I was worn down and exhausted from constantly living in survival mode. His vitality was contagious. It inspired a second wind within my tired, aging self. The things that I was shy or hesitant about, he was bold and courageous about. The things that he stumbled over or needed prompting to bring out, I was ready and willing to unlock. This kept a youthful, childlike wonder alive between us.

Greg's Hesitancy: Guarding His Heart

Greg and I had been seeing each other for a couple of weeks when we faced a serious moment of truth. One night, while lying in bed after a good conversation, things were building up for us to share an intimate moment. Suddenly, the gravity of what being intimate again would mean for us became painfully apparent.

A serious look came over Greg's face. He said there was something important to discuss before he could go any further. I was confused about what could possibly be so important for him to pump the breaks. This wasn't the Greg I was used to, the one who always dove headfirst with reckless abandon into lovemaking.

Before I had time to prepare myself for what he'd say next, he came right out and asked what my intentions were. He wanted to know if this was a casual fling for me or if it was serious. His heart couldn't bear being strung along. The way I had gone about leaving him to start our separation period (by using the news that I was seeing someone else) was the most painful heartache he'd ever experienced.

"I can't go through that again," he said.

Greg went on to express what our love meant to him and how he wanted to treat it with the sanctity and respect it deserved. It was clear he had given some serious thought to our relationship over the years and dedicated himself to growing from the person he was before.

I was taken aback that my former lover, known for his primal, passionate lust, showed such restraint. The tables had finally turned. Now, he was the one thinking things through and listening to his heart, while I was quickly going through the motions and eager to let things ride.

I didn't know how to answer him in that moment, but I knew what I wanted. The only response I managed was to confirm that I still loved him, too, with the same intensity as before. Satisfied with my answer but still noticeably hesitant, Greg let his guard down, and our night resumed.

Sleeping with him had always been a magical experience. But that night, there was a special feeling of pure enchantment. The endless thirst for one another that had been dormant for so long revived like a phoenix rising from the ashes.

A Touch that Transcends Reality

Physical intimacy with a Twin Flame is unlike any sexual experience you've ever had. Being intimate with someone you don't have a soul connection is just sex. You only feel the physical bond between you and, if you're lucky, some alignment of your auric (electromagnetic) energies.

With your Twin Flame, you're interacting not only physically but spiritually, too. Your actions in the 3D are mirrored and amplified by your connection to them in the 5D. Higher vibrational sex puts the pleasure they'd get from material-world intimacy to shame.

When I run my fingers through my Twin Flame's hair or graze my hand down his torso, feeling the softness of his skin and warmth of his body, I don't just feel the physical sensation. I'm in another place in my mind. I tend to not look at what I'm doing and close my eyes to feel—feel him close to me, feel him become excited by this since it's not the typical type of touching.

A deep energy is transferred, slipping past the ego and penetrating each energetic layer of his self. As this is occurs, the silver cord that connects our higher selves playfully tugs at the solar plexus, bringing our energy centers into alignment. By this point, the sensation he receives from my touch cannot be described in words. We've surpassed the limitations of the English language. *This* is how Twin Flames show intimacy.

I'd forgotten the magic we'd known from the relationship we had years before. My focus on the illusions of the material world had overridden my faith in the universe's limitless possibilities. All the things I had to get done for work, for my daughter, for my home blanketed my being in a mundane, colorless net that smothered my dreams and passions. This was no match for Twin Flame Love, though. The magic was being reborn.

Over the next few months of our journey, I felt my spirit come back into my body. Greg wrapped me in a golden blanket of universal love that healed and revived my heart. The panic in my chest subsided, my hands stopped shaking, and my breath became fuller. It was fated, spiritually inscribed into our soul contracts, for us to come back together.

We were coming up on the three-month mark of our rekindled relationship. Historically, it's a time that meant trouble for us. Around the third month, the bursting flare of excitement starts to dim. The dimming light casts shadows for inner insecurities and doubts to lurk, and fear takes hold.

False Evidence Appearing Real (FEAR)

Fear, or **f**alse **e**vidence **a**ppearing **r**eal, loves to ravage the mind with torturous thoughts of "what if?" It causes a snowflake of small doubt to snowball into a full-fledged abominable ice creature whose only reason for existing is to send us deeper into panic, anxiety, and terror.

The mind then projects these thoughts onto the situation's potential outcomes and continues obsessing with its fearful questions, falling further into panic from the lack of a concrete answer.

One finds that they're reinventing and reliving future possibilities over and over, living in a narrative of anxiety about what *could* be. All for a future that hasn't even come into reality yet, so nothing is *actually* wrong.

That's what was going on with Greg and me. The energy of our doubts and insecurities was reflected onto the other like a vicious feedback loop. The unhealed trauma, old patterns, and damage of our past were taking over. This low-frequency energy manifested into dysfunction and distortion in the relationship.

Greg's insecurity over my relationship with my husband (who I was separated from but still legally married to) to coparent our daughter and his fear that I might go back to my marriage began to take hold. His questions about my loyalty brought up old emotions in me. It was reminiscent of the hurtful way he'd acted on his fears in the past. Would he repeat our first relationship and sleep with someone else to compensate?

My fear that Greg might relapse into the behavior of the past grew to infect my view of the future. It clouded my ability to see our potential possibilities together through a lens other than worry and uncertainty. For instance, Greg hadn't set up his life yet and was just getting his footing in sobriety. My life was in an upheaval. I was in the process of relocating, newly laid off from work, taking the first steps toward divorce, rediscovering myself, and coming to terms with raising my daughter as a single mother. There were so many unknowns that we could've braved together if fear hadn't taken hold.

What You Focus on Grows

What you focus on grows.

Let me say that again: **What you focus on grows,** and your thoughts become things.

I got an intuitive feeling that Greg wouldn't live into old age. I didn't trust in my intuition or metaphysical things yet. I still needed physical proof or rational logic to accept something as truth. This made it difficult to decide what to do with this intuitive information. Should I pursue a serious relationship with him, knowing we'd have limited time together? Or should I succumb to the fear of having a broken heart when he dies and I'm still here, living the rest of my days alone?

I also had a strange feeling that if we *did* try to stay together and make it work, it wouldn't be possible until he was forty years old (Spoiler alert: Keep this age in mind!). That was eight years away—a long time that I didn't want to struggle to be with him or have to go through another separation stage to get to.

I wanted forever. I was scared to get attached to him, scared for him to assume a father-like role in my young daughter's life only to leave us when he passed away. I was in a state of decision paralysis, overthinking and allowing what *could* be to rule my life rather than living my life based on what *was*. Fear was taking over my life.

I thought, "How selfish am I to turn down spending valuable years together as if it's not enough because I'm afraid of what might come after?"

No matter the series of events I figured out or the combinations of possibilities I hypothesized, I couldn't see any path to a secure and stable future together. Perhaps I subconsciously closed myself off to it and let my fear blind me. Or maybe I wasn't able to get any sense of having a long-term life with Greg because it was already written in the Book of Life that he would die just twenty months later.

"I'm Going to Marry You."

However, Greg had a different perspective. His ideas about the future were fueled by his heart, not his fears. His heart was so sweet and optimistically hopeful—he was a true believer that love is all that's needed to get by. He believed we were meant to be together with every fiber of his being.

He often looked me dead in the eyes and said, "I'm going to marry you."

I wanted to believe he was just indulging in his fantastical dreams. But he wasn't kidding. He was 100% convinced that he would marry me one day. What he said and the way he said it with such conviction stuck with me. I dog-eared these moments in my memory, as if I knew it would be important for the future.

His passionate conviction that we'd attain the happily-ever-after we dreamed of so many years ago wasn't enough to sway the nagging feeling in my gut. Instead of responding to his notions of being together forever with something like, "It's not meant to be," I said something that struck me as odd.

"We're not meant for this life," I told him.

Notice that I said, "for *this* life," as if there was another life that we were meant to be together. Did I have a spiritual Freudian slip, where my higher self influenced my word choice to leave it open-ended for other lives? Say, the life of someone who embodies a different fragment of my Twin Flame's soul?

The Final Weeks

Greg left in the fall of 2020 to go out of town to tend to his addiction recovery for three months. I used this time to close out what remained of my marriage. I never got to tie up loose ends with my estranged husband because Greg had crashed into my life so quickly. This created tons of tension between Greg and me, but I was finally able to wrap things up with Mike and could move forward in my Twin Flame journey.

The three months were up, and Greg returned home as planned in January. The first thing I noticed was his shaggy long hair. I had a funny thought and let out a laugh.

"What're you laughing about?" He asked.

"I don't want to say it out loud because it's kind of morbid." I replied.

He eventually coaxed it out of me, and I said, "You gotta cut your hair because, God forbid, if something were to happen, I don't want my memory of you to change... I don't want to remember you looking like a pirate!"

The seriousness of my statement was not lost in the comical way I said it. He took my words to heart and cut his hair as if his spirit subliminally told him to be mindful of the truth in my words.

A Gift of REBIRTH

Greg decided to show his devotion to his recovery and to our relationship by surprising me with two necklaces. One was a mother/daughter necklace with a charm depicting two intertwined hearts. On the back, it was inscribed with the message, "Forever connected at heart." It was a gift that signified his connection with my young daughter, Everly, and his admiration for the family bond.

The second necklace had me perplexed. The packaging displayed the title "REBIRTH" in large capital letters printed above the necklace. The necklace was gold, which was an unusual choice since Greg knew I preferred silver (Another spoiler: Gold would become significant). The necklace had a large circular charm with a twelve-petal lotus and a green jade stone at the center of the lotus blossom. I'd later conduct research to discover that the twelve-petal lotus represents the heart chakra and the spiritual rebirth one experiences throughout the journey of enlightenment.

According to AnthroWiki's article on the heart chakra, "The 12-petalled lotus flower opens up insights that reach the level of intuition. It is the main sense of intuition through which, among other things, retrospection into previous incarnations becomes possible."

The article goes on to explain something about soul transformation: "In order for the heart chakra to become consciously active, the sentient soul must be transformed into the intuitional soul."

Greg and I never discussed pseudospiritual concepts or anything relating to spiritual transformation, reincarnation, or rebirth, so to receive this lotus necklace from him just days before he died stands out as unusual.

My ego wondered if maybe I was fooling myself into seeing a deeper meaning that wasn't there. I scoured the internet to find where this necklace was sold to see if there was a reason Greg chose this specific design. I found it listed online on a big box store's website. It was part of a series of jewelry that offered themes like love; I'm sure he saw these other options. But no. He chose "REBIRTH" as his gift to me.

Individually, events, occurrences, and synchronicities like these don't hold meaning. But taken into context together, they illuminate the invisible thread that life plays out on. Once you start to see the path outlined by these points of connection, the insights gained from seeing this thread enable you to steer in whatever direction you desire.

In the case of the lotus flower necklace, the jewelry itself was not what was profound. Neither was the act of Greg gifting it to me or the message of rebirth it contained. Its significance is that it acted as a material beacon of light to signal greater things. It stood out to me so much that it cut through the distractions of daily life and brought the focus back to what would lead me to my higher good.

What I once perceived as random and trivial became relevant and consequential when viewed in the greater context of life's direction. For instance, Greg also gave me a large quartz crystal wrapped in thick copper wire. It surprised me that he'd wrapped it himself. I'd never known him to be interested in crystals or wire wrapping. Today, this holds a ton of meaning because of what I've learned about the conductivity of copper wire and metaphysical principles of crystal healing.

Embeddings: Deeper Meanings

The connections between the things you do, the people you love, and the situations you find yourself in reveal an entangled network at work in your life.

The human mind is known for its ability for pattern recognition, but *this* level of detection is much different. Your mental body doesn't perceive this level of information. These types of embeddings are recognized through other channels, like your heart's intuition. If you have to actively search for something's meaning, that's not the kind of connection I'm referring to.

You can tell a point of connection or *embedding* from a regular day-to-day event if it activates your intuition. Something in you tells you notice what you're experiencing, though you're not quite sure why. Later down the road, something clicks, and you'll realize the synchronicity. This discovery is extremely satisfying because you discover the truth you were meant to.

Piecing these points of connection together and keeping an eye out for life's embeddings is like removing the dam that was clunking up the river of your thoughts, feelings, and being. Everything flows smoother and easier.

It's evidence that life is not the random collection of chaotic, meaningless events that some want you to believe it is. Piecing these events together brings feelings of relief, assurance, and greater confidence in yourself that what you're experiencing and what you know in your heart was right all along.

Phil's Passing

The closer the time got to Greg's passing, the more pronounced the points of connection became and the more frequently they occurred.

Just four days before Greg's death, my father-in-law, Phil, passed away. Phil died on Monday, and then Greg died that Friday. If there was ever a week of the year that signified endings, it would be this one. (This occurred during the peak of the COVID-19 pandemic, which led to many spiritual awakenings across the globe. I won't go into that topic but do want to note it to provide context to the timeline.)

My husband's father, Phil, had been instrumental in the success of my marriage in prior years. He was the voice of understanding and reason. So when he died, I knew right then and there that my marriage was officially over. Not because of the ego war between Greg and my husband. Not because of the damage caused by Mike's desertion of our daughter and me. Phil's death carried the energetic weight of "the end of a cycle."

My marriage was over, but I'd never get to freely explore things with Greg like we both had planned together.

Chapter 8

"He Is Dead"

January 6, 2021. Yes, that was the day when a group of protestors stormed the White House in Washington, DC. It's also the day Greg returned home after being away for three months. Sixteen days later, on January 22, another pivotal event occurred.

For late January, the 22nd was mildly warm and sunny. Greg and I spent the previous night arguing via text message—I can't even remember what about. I dropped my daughter off at daycare that morning and took a walk to decompress at the nearby park.

I looked at my phone right as a text from Greg came through. It was 10:07 a.m. The tone of the conversation hadn't improved from the night before, so I turned my attention to the beautiful nature trail and continued walking.

A Shift of Energy

I was walking along the trail, thinking about the workday ahead of me, when, out of nowhere, my intuition flared up. Energetic alarm bells went off—something big was happening. I stopped walking to get a better read on what it was. I looked upward and noticed the tall trees towering overhead. The sky was clear, and the air was crisp.

"This feeling isn't physical," I thought.

It was a type of energy activation, like what I felt the first time I laid eyes on Greg over a decade earlier, when the world around us paused and an electric feeling filled the air. Energy was transferring and transforming. I took note of the odd moment and resumed my walk home.

Around 10:22 a.m., I felt an even more intense surge of energy. It was so powerful that it stopped me right in my tracks. It was oddly familiar, but I had no clue what it was.

Three hours later, Greg's mother sent me a text message with three simple words: "He is dead." It had taken some time for Greg's body to be discovered. EMT estimated his time of death around the same time that I felt that energetic shift.

The moment my mind processed these words, I knew that my life was forever changed. Just as it'd been forever changed thirteen years ago when he first entered my life.

A Karmic Incarnation

When a Twin Flame passes away, the moment of their departure is likely preplanned. It was agreed on in your soul contract and etched into the fiber of your being before you were born. Your higher self chose to experience their death. It was agreed upon in your soul contract before either of you were born.

The reason you agreed to this might be to assist in your growth or have to do with reasons unrelated to the Twin Flame mission like breaking a karmic cycle. Regardless of the reason, a Twin Flame who dies never leaves their surviving counterpart. They're by their mate's side 24/7 to help them actualize their purpose.

I often think about why Greg died when he did. He was physically fit, healthy, and had a fighting spirit. It doesn't make sense that he'd suddenly tap out of life. I looked to contextual details over the greater picture and realized that he was here to play a supporting role for others and to use his thirty-three years to balance his karma.

His task was to remove the karmic baggage that was weigh-ing him down so he could break free of his karmic cycles. Once he achieved this, his mission was complete, and he passed away. I'd like to think he knew he accomplished his calling, hence why his fighting spirit let go and allowed him to pass at the specific time it did.

A karmic lifetime also comes with complications of the ego, of pain that another person can never resolve. I felt like no mat-ter what I did, I could never get to the source of Greg's pain. Nothing in his lifetime could have caused such a wound. It was carried over from other incarnations.

All in all, Greg's death was the ultimate show of love. The ultimate sacrifice. He died so I could live the life I'm leading now.

Keriah

Have you ever noticed how your life follows a certain pattern, where specific dates or times of year seem to be eventful each year? Dates like February 8 and August 26 never fail to be signif-icant for me. February 8, 2002, was my thirteenth birthday party, where I met my best friend who put me on the trajectory to meet Greg. In the true spirit of connectivity and synchronicity, February 8, 2021, also proved to be profound.

February 8th, eighteen days after Greg died and two days af-ter what would've been his 34th birthday, I woke up feeling like I was being hugged. Like he was there, holding me. I felt the pres-ence of my Twin Flame as if he was living and breathing in phys-ical form. But the human part of me, the part that craved to be close to him in the 3D world, still missed him terribly. I expressed this in my journal:

I swear, I can still remember how you feel, as if you're still here physically. The way your bare skin feels on my cheek when I'd lay my head on your chest, the sound of your heart-beat, the sensation I'd get when we're so still that I can bask

I decided to take a walk at the park by my house. The same trail I was on when I felt the energetic shift of his passing. My intuition guided me to take the same route I walked the day he died and repeat my same steps. I turned on a streaming app on my phone to listen to music. I'd just installed it. I hadn't yet built up a repertoire of songs or given the app the chance to gather data to adapt its algorithm to my preferences. When I reached the spot on the trail where I was when I received the last text message I'd ever get from Greg, the song "Purpose" by Justin Bieber came on.

I thought it was odd for this song to play because the playlist was supposed to be rock and electronica. "Purpose" was not in either of these genres. Aside from what I'd heard on the radio, I'd never listened to Justin Bieber before. This song was six years old by that point, too, so it wasn't like the streaming app was trying to promote it.

The song started with a sentimental piano ballad—completely different from the upbeat pop tones this artist is known for. The opening lyric of the song immediately caught my attention. It recounted the tale of the singer's life in grace and appreciation, as if it was an open love letter to the Divine. It told of the struggles he'd endured and exhibited the raw pain he felt. The vibrations of the song rang through the airwaves and hit me as if it was Greg himself reciting the words to me. In that moment, I felt the frequency of miracles.

I stopped walking and stood there, under a cloudless blue sky, motionlessly taking it all in. The trail was surrounding an open grassy field with a lush, green forest in the distance. The trees were old and well-established, like they'd been standing tall for generations and generations, all the while witnessing the events of human history play out before them. Like they held ancient knowledge and sacred wisdom from their time as silent observers. Their branches rested multiple stories high up into the bright cyan sky. I felt this land was special to previous generations in some way, to people I'd never meet but who had the same sense of gratitude I was feeling now.

The song continued to ring out from my phone's speakers. With each line of lyrical magic came an emotional blow to my grieving soul. It was painful yet healing and comforting at the same time.

With every fiber of my being, I knew that Greg was using this song to speak to me. The events of life—including waking up that day feeling Greg's phantom embrace, returning to the park, and deciding to play the streaming app and have this particular song come on—all culminated to bring me to this moment with purposeful intention.

The message of the song rocked me at my core. It represented the pain Greg felt from his inner struggle to cope with the consequences of his wrongdoings. He was working to correct the mistakes of his past and live a life as expected by society, but the years of being off the beaten path wore him down. Dimmed the light in his soul. Greg struggled to live his life, plagued by the consequences of these mistakes that didn't accurately reflect who he was. This song, "Purpose," emanated that pain.

My legs gave out, and I fell to the ground. It was a true Keriah moment (Keriah is the Hebrew tradition of tearing one's clothes in an expression of mourning, grief, and loss). I burst into tears, fell to the ground, and sobbed.

I was at the top of the trail by the park entrance near a busy road. The vibration of the multi-ton vehicles rumbled through the ground and up my body as they drove by. I remained there, kneeling on the ground for the duration of the three-minute-long song. I was visible for all the cars and passersby to see. They probably thought it was strange, but I didn't care. I was experiencing something momentous.

I looked up at the sky through the tears in my eyes and thanked Greg for helping me to understand his pain. It was a powerful moment of mixed emotions. I felt the rawness of Greg's pain, the sorrow of my loss, the grace of blessing and awareness, and the incredible wonder of synchronicity. I proceeded to thank God for creating a world that allowed me to connect to my loved one at this level.

Through this experience, I realized that Greg considered me to be his *purpose*. His time with me was the closest he'd felt to having a place in the world. I was eternally grateful for everything I experienced with him. The lessons learned, the things encountered, and the love shared was breathing new life into my soul.

I regained my composure after being reduced to a big ball of tears and replayed the song on my walk back. Right when it reached the chorus, I felt the wind pick up. The light breeze softly caressed my face as if it was Greg consoling me, urging me to stop crying. I could almost feel the touch of his hand wipe the tears away from my cheek.

As I arrived back at my car, I expressed a heartfelt confession to Greg:

> *You truly are my purpose. I clearly see all the points of connection in our journey and understand why each event had to happen to lead us here. Was I really so stupid to <u>not</u> see that I had the love of all my lifetimes right in front of me the whole time? Why did I resist you so much? Well, that might've been because you were a lot for me to handle. But no matter how overwhelming things got, I never stopped wanting you in my life. I miss you every day. But instead of emanating a feeling of sadness or pity, I choose to radiate the warmth of the love you and I share. That is your legacy.*

I recorded my message to Greg on my phone and documented it for perspective. It's easy to look back on a relationship with rose-colored glasses, especially if the person has passed away. Memory is fallible. It's influenced by current moods and beliefs, and can change over time. Documentation can provide the insight needed to counter this fallibility and remember things with accuracy.

For example, I didn't realize until I reviewed my decade-old journal entries and letters from Greg that cycles were occurring each year in January and July. These cycles were characterized by extreme highs and troubling lows, as well as other significant events. I learned more information about the cycles by looking at numerology and tools like The Pattern app. This revealed tons of great insight that helped put our past behavior into perspective. Without the documentation of events, it would've been difficult to confirm the existence of these cycles or learn how to grow from them by memory alone.

There were certain times when the energy is stronger than usual—like in the January cycle. Here's a journal entry I wrote over ten years ago in January that shows this:

> *Why did I have to go through all of this pain? How much more suffering was I going to have to go through before you'd take the steps to change?*
>
> *I am trying to grow, and the next step for me is forgiveness. I'm not over the pain you've caused, but am trying my best with this: I forgive you, Greg.*
>
> *Maybe one day we'll meet again. Hopefully by then I won't be already married and moved on. I love you. Good luck.*

The energy in this entry was certainly high, but my sentiment was much different from the post-death declaration of my love to him.

Another Look at the Mayan Calendar

The ancient Mayan calendar debate of 2012 reminds us to consider the cycles we're in. The Maya people were aware of life's cyclical nature. They recognized cycles at personal, global, and universal levels, and observed the natural repetition and connection. We can take a page from the Maya's example and reflect on the events in our lives to identify the patterns and cycles we're in.

A major cycle in my Twin Flame journey—the start of my separation period from Greg—occurred in 2012. So, if what the Maya have to say about cycles is right, it makes perfect sense that the universe is affected by these invisible cycles. Also, the Mayan Long Count calendar concluded with December 21, 2021. The date of Gregory's death was January 22, 2021.

When the numbers of these dates are written out in consequential order, I the similarity is uncanny:

- January 22, 2021 (1/22/2021):   112222
- December 21, 2012 (12/21/2021):   1112222

Cycles and Patterns

As with everything in life, the Twin Flame journey is cyclical. Cycles aren't usually easy to notice. There isn't a hard starting or stopping point to a cycle. Cycles can overlap and revolve concurrently, making it hard to tell what's what. But you can identify a cycle by looking at your circumstances, situations, and relationships for patterns.

Consider what's going on in the background, such as planetary positions, cosmic currents, and other things you might not normally keep track of. When you're mindful of the things that are happening beyond the surface level, you gain the awareness to dissect past situations and understand *why* things unfolded the way they did.

Detecting these patterns enables you to identify cycles as they are happening rather than in retrospect. If you realize you're in a cycle, you can adjust your response to achieve the outcome you're aiming for. Look at how you handled things in the past, and analyze your behavior see where you can grow and how you can handle the situation differently.

Or if you continually find yourself faced with the same type of situation over and over again, perhaps there's a lesson you're meant to learn and wisdom to implement.

Sometimes, simply learning the lesson isn't enough. Simply knowing what the lesson is doesn't leave a big-enough mark on the universe for things to change. *Action* is required to bring your newfound knowledge to fruition. You've got to show the universe that the lesson was learned and apply it in your actions. Doing so is to speak the universe's language of creation. Only then will you break the cycle.

The Dawn of a Spiritual Renewal

Greg's death catapulted me onto a path of spiritual renewal. I felt an energetic window open. All the energies aligned, and I was in the right place in my life to see it. I jokingly refer to the cataclysmic effects that Greg's Spirit had as my "spiritual cheat code." Anytime I focused on the love I felt for him, I was thrown into a higher frequency.

I became hypersensitive to the energy around me and receptive to messages from Spirit. I was spotting synchronicities left and right that I'd missed in the past. Signs that pointed towards my destined life path had been all around me well before Greg died. My focus before his death distracted me from seeing them.

Before, my vision of the 5D was clouded, with dim light cast from far off in the distance and blurred by the fog. Now, it was like a supernova had burst into bright beams of light that reached every aspect of my life. The light illuminated the things from my past and lifted key pieces of information out of the darkness.

The events of my past suddenly made sense, and it was clear how everything fit together. The bigger picture was being revealed. Like putting together a puzzle, you can't make out what picture the puzzle makes until you've put enough of the pieces together for it to begin to take shape.

Chapter 9

Death Is Not an End, Death Is a Transformation

In the weeks after Greg's passed, I found myself in the midst of an energetic transformation. Realizing that Greg's energy was still playing a role in my life, I embraced it. Sure enough, I had another profound interaction with him on March 9 (3/9)—forty-seven days after his death, which reduces to eleven the Twin Flame number.

I said to him in my mind's eye:

"Greg, you've been trying to get my attention for two days now. Tonight, I'm as emotionally wide open, receptive, and in pain as I was when I got my tattoo to commemorate you. I feel an ocean of emotions—a pain felt at every level of my soul—but one that I know must be felt to receive whatever lessons and blessings are to come. Yesterday, you seemed to be either trying to get my attention in an urgent way or to be playful. Today, I can feel you with me, but am a bit down because I don't know if I remember what you look like right now."

Immediately after completing that thought, I heard, "Baby, you know what I look like," through the ether.

The words entered my mind just as my own conscious thought would, but they were formed perfectly in his voice and manner, as if he was alive.

"See? You even know what I sound like [since you're receiving this message and hearing me now]," he added.

My mind created a mental picture of us standing together. In this mental image, I fell into his arms and clasped my hands around his waist. My head leaned on his shoulder. I squeezed him tight to feel a sense of safety and stability. He wrapped his arms around me, holding me just as tightly in return. In that moment, I relived the feeling of completeness I got from being in his arms.

Then, the memory of our first kiss resurfaced. I watched it play out in my mind like a movie being projected onto the theater screen. We were at his house, sitting on his bed, watching a movie on DVD. As I replayed this moment in my mind, I questioned whether I was watching my memory of it or his. How strange to suddenly have that pop into my head! Reliving memories served the dual purpose of processing the unresolved emotion from the experiences and igniting the sense of universal love the events emanated.

When I felt the presence of his energy around me, it was as if Greg was physically there with me. But I'd also feel his presence quickly fade away, too. It was similar to how someone exits a room, like he was going to visit his other family and friends on the material plane. While I knew he wasn't doing this to deprive me of time with him or to withhold love from me, my ego couldn't help but wonder why he didn't *stay* with me.

When I thought these negative thoughts, he quickly corrected me: "If you would've focused on the positive, you would've realized I was waiting to come back and give you the same."

From there, I was sent into a moment where I remembered how his hair used to feel, tickling my torso as he moved about my body to kiss and caress me. The memory turned lucid, and I looked toward him to catch his gaze. He said to me, "I love you."

I felt my world shift *again* and the next thing I knew, we were floating in a space-like realm. There were visuals of vivid rainbows and colors. It was vibrant, calm, and happy all at the same time.

Greg's physical presence wasn't required for me to bring this feeling to life. Greg's love and the energy of his soul were all I needed thanks to this connection that seemed to transcend reality itself. This feeling I'd missed so much in my grief was no longer a pipe dream. It was no longer distant. It was no longer missed because it was *real*.

All I could think was how wrong I was when I told him we weren't meant for this life.

The Promise of Rebirth

At the end of a major life cycle and on the cusp of a new one beginning, I received a promise that I would continue the Twin Flame journey in this lifetime. This promise came to me intuitively, like a thought I would think to myself, but more powerfully. I confirmed the validity of this promise with my Spirit guides, who I learned to work with in meditation after Greg died, and by what felt like everywhere I looked in life.

At first, I shrugged it off as my mind's way of dealing with the grief. Could I really expect to embark on the same Twin Flame journey with not one but two different people in this lifetime? Since Twin Flames are connected at the soul and not the physical body, the question became, is it possible to find his soul in this world again?

Answers to these questions came flooding in through my intuition, synchronicities, and the messages delivered by others. I slowly started to believe that it was possible. After all, when Greg passed away, my connection to him didn't fade. It grew stronger. And if that was possible, then was what I was being promised so farfetched?

Part of me had trouble accepting it as a real possibility. I had to make the conscious choice to trust that what's mine will never pass me by. I worked to remove limitations in my perception, break cycles, shed old habits, and heal things within myself so I could accept the impossible as possible.

The events leading up to Greg's death, from our initial meeting to separation and everything in between, *had* to happen. His death was etched into our soul contract, agreed upon before we were born. It wasn't some unfortunate event born out of chaos. This gave me comfort and hope. It fueled my faith that our higher selves knew where this would lead.

Rather than focus on the physical loss, I put my attention on the universal love and extraordinary connection that seemed to transcend dimensional realities right before my eyes and support me in reaching my intended life path. I chose to surrender to the flow of the universe and trust the process.

My Twin Flame always loved to challenge the impossible, so I knew he was up for the task of bringing this miracle to fruition.

Death and Grief

The weather was stormy outside, and my four-year-old daughter was deep in thought. She seemed concerned about something.

After moments of silence, she asked, "Mommy, I'm scared of tornados. Have I been in one before?"

"No, you haven't," I assured her. "There's nothing to worry about. It's just a storm."

"But Mom, you told me we've had a tornado before."

"Yes, 'we,' as in our hometown, had a tornado, but it was a long time ago. Before you were even born," I said.

"Before... I was... born?" she stuttered. You could see the wheels turning in her head as she tried to grasp this. "So, I was *dead*?"

I was caught off guard by hearing it put so bluntly. "Well, you weren't born yet and weren't alive. So, yes, I guess you were *dead*."

Her lack of reaction to my response was surprising. She wasn't confused, perplexed, or even startled by the idea that she was "dead" before she was alive. She seemed comfortable with the idea, like it made sense and wasn't something to fear.

This conversation with my young daughter raised an excellent point. We only say someone is dead when referring to the period after that person's body has died. But what about the period before their soul arrived here on Earth? Are they dead then?

If we refer to an era of time before we were born, like ancient Rome or the Great Depression, we don't refer to ourselves as being dead. We say that we weren't born yet. But if you think about it, we're dead *before* we enter our bodies. If there's life after death, then there's life before it, too.

I wasn't overrun with grief when Greg died because I didn't define Greg as his physical body. If Greg were only his physical presence, then the energy of his love for me would've faded when his body perished. But that's not what happened.

The part of his soul that resided in his body returned to his higher self, into his true, pure self, and my higher self was right there alongside him outside of time.

Knowing that we were in the other's presence in Spirit and feeling his love continue to flow to me made it impossible for grief to take hold. After all, how can you grieve someone's death when they're very much alive?

Our DNA is already ingrained with these truths, including the inherent wisdom to know better than to cry over spilled milk (the physical loss of someone you love) when the whole dairy farm (a connection to their eternal soul energy) is just across the way!

Before Greg died, my only experience with the death of a loved one was my Pappy, back when I was four years old (Greg's mother pointed out the connection that Everly was four when Greg passed). For me to be a stranger to death and process my Twin Flame's passing in such a productive way is a miracle on its own.

The Metaphysics of Rebirth

My Spirit guides made it very clear that the purpose of my Twin Flame's return wouldn't only be to fulfill my romantic desire. His return was necessary for me to achieve my life purpose. But for Greg to rejoin my life as a grown adult near my same age, he'd have to seemingly defy time.

The process by which he would come back might be less of a return and more of an activation. He'd need to either integrate his soul into a human body at the time of their birth (which would have happened many years ago, and his soul energy would technically be operating in "sleeper status" until the moment of activation that would collide with my timeline years later) or make an agreement with a fellow soul in the 5D to activate or "walk in" now via their body here. This is what is called a walk-in soul situation.

Since the soul is independent of the body, it has the flexibility of when and how it chooses to enter its human form. Let's say Greg has a buddy, Sam, who he's formed a trusting bond with over the past incarnations they've shared. Sam is currently living a human life in the same period as Greg's death. In today's time, Sam is a grown adult with an established life on Earth. Greg could ask Sam's soul (higher self) to lend him a favor and use Sam's body to host Greg's soul for a while. Sam will still be Sam, physically, but Greg's soul energy will shine through and be unmistakable to those who know it.

What seems impossible to us here on Earth, like what's described above, is entirely possible when we consider it as it would be perceived from the 5D. However, something like this couldn't be accomplished by my or Greg's efforts alone. It'd require a team effort between myself, Greg's Spirit, our soul family, and God.

Coming to Earth requires energy; so does activating one's soul. Both methods take a lot of energy to pull off—more than the average soul possesses alone. The energy has to come from somewhere. For Greg to return, multiple members of our soul family must work together to make it possible. He couldn't do it if the other souls in our network disagreed or thought it was a poor decision.

Given Greg's stubbornness to be steadfast in what he believes is right, I had full confidence that he could convince them to aid his endeavor. I could see him using his clever skills to rationally present his argument to our guides, persuading them that it's a good idea to work with him to facilitate his return. Knowing Greg's fighting spirit, I couldn't imagine him *not* taking the opportunity to return to this world.

Communication Through Spirit Guides

It's important to build your relationship with your guide(s) as you would with any other lifelong friend. The more you know them, the more confidence you'll have in what they send you. It'll be easier to understand how they word things, their sense of humor, and how they get your attention for the big "life-path level" matters versus the smaller day-to-day things.

Sometimes, I just pal around with my guide and engage in playful banter. He presents himself as a middle-aged man with a heavy Roman accent. This appearance was chosen because we shared a past life together in 34 A.D. Rome, where he was my paternal figure (Greg was actually my sibling in that lifetime!). A fatherly persona is a wise choice to ensure I hold the information he conveys is held in high regard.

The Guide/soul relationship is very much like the father/child one, where the father is no "better" than the child in terms of superiority, but the child heeds their father's words because they're being said from a place of wisdom, prudence, and universal love. A child appreciates fatherly advice and cherishes it more than if it came from someone else.

At every step of the process toward reuniting, I checked in with my Spirit guides in meditation and used my intuition to connect with them throughout my day. I also ensured that what I was do-ing didn't go against God. Everything I did, I did with a perception that God is the ultimate Creator and that nothing is above him.

I practiced prayer and gave gratitude to God for allowing me to know Him so intimately as to lend my mere human self the divine gifts of energetic abilities like manifestation and telepathy. This acknowledgement was critical. Without it, I'd misattribute the amazing things I was seeing as being of my own doing or, even sadder, something that occurred by meaningless chance.

Even in moments where I had little to no clue of what I was experiencing, like the intense out-of-body meditations and en-ergy activations, keeping God as the ultimate Almighty One kept me secure, grounded, and stable. It tethered me to something greater than anything I'd encounter here on Earth and freed me to dive into the unknown without fear of being led astray.

Faith as a Grounding Tool

Everything in the universe is vibrating and oscillating in a constant state of motion. Even our thoughts resonate at a spe-cific vibrational frequency. Humans are equipped with the en-ergy fields and functions needed to vibrate with (or against) the things in our universe, and that is how we co-create, manifest, and affect things. God designed us to be *co-creators* with our universe.

It's a blessing to live during the dawn of the Age of Aquarius, a time that happens to be the point in human history where we understand the basics of the quantum universe. Our under-standing of the human body and consciousness as it exists in relation to the vibrational universe is growing. We're coming into harmony with the world around us.

As you explore new schools of thought and as you consume more information to discern your own beliefs, ground yourself in something greater. Don't allow something of man to be regarded as higher or greater than the Higher Power, even if you're not founded in a belief of any particular religion.

Chapter 10

Getting Into Alignment: Doing the Inner Work

While I waited for what needed to happen on Spirit's side to bring about this divine promise, I went to work on getting up to spec and aligning myself with a miracle. I used every day to work on transcending my ego, opening my heart, and getting in tune with the universe's signals so I'd be ready when the time came for my Twin Flame to return.

If I wanted to find my Twin Flame again, I'd have to fully accept the idea of limitless possibility. I'd have to trust in that 100%. For six months after Greg's death, I did everything in my power to remove the barriers that held me back from finding my "new" counterpart. Every day was an opportunity to grow closer to my miracle by learning, growing, healing, and connecting.

Why Starting with the Self Is So Effective

All aspects of life come together to form your current state. Your inner state affects your outer state, and vice versa. To receive the love that I dreamt of, I'd have to match the vibration I was calling in and emanate it from within. I supported my personal transformation (my inner state) by transforming my environment (my outer state).

In my living space, I created designated areas of reprieve for days when getting outside in nature to clear my mind wasn't possible. These spaces were outfitted with high-vibrational crystals, sentimental paintings from local artists, and other products of love, dedication, and good intention. Pillows, candles, and other accents were added for comfort. I experimented with using sage and therapeutic aromas like eucalyptus and sandalwood.

The goal was to make my space into a physical embodiment of what I wanted my inner self to be—high vibrational and conducive to the limitless possibilities I was being promised. A place I'd *want* to spend time in rather to escape from. I gave myself no reason to feel flustered or overwhelmed in my own home.

The improvements in my external environment fed back into my inner state. It supported an openness to an appreciation, gratitude, and universal love that I could embody within myself and extend to others. The effort to clear, set, and align all aspects of my life was coming together.

Universal Love → New Earth

For Twin Flames, universal love is not a fairy-tale concept that would be nice if we could find it. This type of pure, infinite love is already written into our DNA. Even *that* is a miraculous thought.

Can you imagine what the world would be like if you loved an acquaintance or coworker as universally as you love your Twin Flame? It'd be an entirely different world! (Maybe "New Earth" aka ascended Earth, perhaps?)

Transforming the Relationship

Greg's transition to Spirit strengthened my connection to the astral and ethereal planes. I took advantage of this and meditated at least once a day to communicate with my guides and Twin Flame, using methods like visualization and astral projection. I'll never forget some of the first messages I received from Greg in meditation, like "You are SO much more than you think," and "I'm going to show you some things."

More on Spirit Guides

Spirit guides act like the faucet that controls the energetic flow between you and the astral, etheric, and other levels. The faucet can be wide open and allow both low- and high-vibrational communications to reach you. Or you can request that it be limited to only high-vibrational. Your guides will help you.

When working with your guides, always verify what you receive. Get confirmation of the message's source. Ask for verification of its origin. For instance, Greg confirms that it's him by sending me a special phrase—a key word that other souls wouldn't know to provide.

Beware of low-vibrational energies. If what you're receiving isn't supportive of your greatest good, ask your Guide to block that level of communication. If what you receive is demeaning, degrading, or puts you down, know that it is not from your Guide, Twin Flame, or soul family. Ask your Guide to limit communication from low-vibrational energies or anything else that's not for your highest good.

I was new to the practice of meditation but tapping into Greg's energy and resonating the frequency of love acted like a catalyst. It accelerated my sessions. Meditation was effortlessly transcendental. In a simple thirty-minute unguided meditation, listening to solfeggio frequencies, I accessed realms that spiritual gurus and masters say take years to reach. This showed me that anyone is capable of higher-level meditation.

I wanted to eliminate any possibility that the emotions from grief, memories, or past beliefs were causing interference with how I interpreted the information I received in meditation. I'd also have to change how I saw Greg and adapt my perception of him to fit his new form. I'd need to "clear the mirror." One of the best ways to do this was through spiritual alchemy.

Spiritual Alchemy

It was time to alchemize past experiences and things that no longer served me. Old energy of memories, trauma, and preconceived notions surrounded me. Feelings and beliefs being distorted by past trauma had to be transmuted to inspired freedom rather than restriction. This would help transform my view of Greg from a romantic partner to a platonic, lifelong helper.

I conducted a personal inventory to identify any unhealthy, limiting beliefs I was holding onto. Some things were engraved at such a deep place in my heart that the chances of pinpointing them were slim to none. I didn't want to cut cords or block something so embedded that doing so might create more harm than good. Instead, I could alchemize them.

Spiritual alchemy uses energy healing to transform existing energy within you into a better state rather than releasing it or cutting cords. It's a great way to transform convoluted pain from childhood or past trauma, like the death of someone you shared a deep relationship with—things that linger in hard-to-reach places within your heart where it's hard to fully surface *all* of it.

The Art of Transmutation

Energy cannot be created or destroyed. Spiritual alchemy allows you to evolve existing energy into something useful instead of wasting that energy by blocking yourself from it.

Your life has been carefully articulated to bring you the people and situations you've experienced, with lessons and life learnings embedded in every piece of your story. If you clear that energy and release it altogether, you might also incidentally release all the wisdom, knowledge, and lessons you gained. Transmuting the energy retains the lessons and knowledge while transforming from low- to high-vibrational energy to support your greatest good.

For instance, the energy of pain or trauma is powerful. Rather than expelling it completely, the heavy, low-vibrational pain from past trauma can be transmuted into uplifting, high-vibrational energy.

It's a good tactic to use in matters of the heart, which can be complicated and stem back to pieces deeply embedded into the fabric of who you are and may not be easily identifiable. Grief can be transmuted into hope. The sinking feeling in the pit of your stomach can be transmuted into healing energy that fills you with an eager zest for life.

One of the biggest lessons I learned when rebirthing the connection with my late Twin Flame is to be careful that your energy isn't prematurely concluding a situation's end, limiting the universe's potential, or stunting its possibilities. While the universe always has your back, it's also constantly inferring your energy to manifest reality. Watch the energetic language you're putting out because the universe is always listening.

Integrating Everything

The past holds valuable lessons and insights we need for growth. That includes the painful ones we'd rather not remember. Disconnecting from these things entirely can cause more harm than good because sometimes, what we infer to be "negative" or "heavy" for us to carry hasn't been fully integrated into our template yet.

It's not as simple as telling yourself, "I'm over it." Integration happens at every level, not just the physical, mental, or emotional ones. It takes a long time to integrate the lessons of an event, too. It could take years for something that happened earlier in your life—before you were ready to take that experience to break cycles and thrive—to fully integrate within you.

I learned this the hard way during my grief journey. While my conscious mind thought, "It's fine... I'm totally healed and over my grief of Greg," the occasional outbursts of emotion when a sentimental song came on or the way he'd invade my dreams begged to differ. There was still something I needed to heal. Something I needed to integrate more fully. Rather than sulking in defeat or feeling like a victim of my grief, I used techniques like the Violet Flame to transmute the lingering energy.

The Violet Flame is a powerful energy tool that burns up even the most stubborn low-vibrational energy. Think of it like a controlled or prescribed burn. Park rangers purposely burn parts of the forest to remove dead foliage, debris, and things that impede the forest's growth. This gets rid of invasive plant species that might carry diseases harmful to indigenous plants. Burning these things rejuvenates the forest and returns it to a state of balance. Using the Violet Flame to manage your spiritual/energetic state is the same.

The Violet Flame

The Violet Flame is a spiritual alchemy tool for transmuting negative energy into positive energy.

One common way to use it is to visualize the Violet Flame surrounding you and filling you with its energy. You can also use mantras, prayers, and affirmations to call forth the Violet Flame. It can be used for many things, including:

- To transmute negative emotions, such as anger, fear, and sadness, into positive emotions like love, joy, and peace.
- To clear negative energy from your aura and chakras.
- To heal physical and emotional wounds.
- To manifest your desires.
- To connect with your higher self and spiritual guides.
- To raise your vibration and consciousness.

Making Room for the New Person

In death, Greg now serves as a **spiritual helper** to my Spirit guides. My perspective of him had to change to match this new role. This was absolutely critical to find the "new" (rebirthed) Twin Flame I'd been promised. If I didn't wholly release my romantic passions for who Greg was, there wouldn't be room for who he could be, and it would make reuniting with him impossible.

The new person who carried Greg's energy would need to be recognized as an individual. Physically, they'd be different from who Greg was. They'd look different, speak differently, and have a different background and upbringing. Carrying over my feelings for Greg would cause issues like disappointment and resentment. Also, the new person could envy my love for Greg and feel like they're second best.

To avoid the pitfall of comparing who I knew my Twin Flame to be to the way he'd show up in the future, I worked through my lingering feelings every day. I kept a gratitude journal, scrapbooked photos for closure, and did Twin Flame Reiki healing sessions I found for free online.

In about three months, my view of Greg had transformed from admiring him as my one-and-only, meant-to-be romantic lover to treasuring him as an eternal, multidimensional companion. This change created space for him to materialize in his new incarnation, free of expectation or comparison, and laid the foundation for a successful reunion.

I didn't need to see him as a lover to know I was loved. I could receive his love in any form, not just the body he had in this lifetime. The love for my Twin Flame extends beyond the boundaries of romantic love. It's something much greater. He wasn't "mine." His soul energy was my resonant match. This is a much different perspective from the typical view of romantic possession.

Strengthening Faith

☑ Environmental
☑ Mental
☑ Emotional
☐ Spiritual

Next on the list of things to transform in preparation for a miracle was the spiritual component. In 2012, eleven years before Greg died, I started a Bible study with my pastor. (The year 2012 keeps popping up, doesn't it?) We met once a week to study the Bible verse by verse for more than a decade.

The understanding that Scripture provided corroborated the metaphysical things I was witnessing—the things I knew in my soul to be true. This is contrary to what some people might assume about the Bible, thinking that it doesn't support mysticism or metaphysics. The Bible encourages humankind to go beyond our single-minded focus and expand to a perspective that incorporates all planes and realms—not just the one we see right before us.

When the disciples first saw Jesus, they were blown away by the idea that they were in the presence of the Messiah. They were so in awe of how amazing this concept was, they couldn't process the simple things Jesus was trying to tell them. There are over twenty instances in the New Testament when the people didn't understand Jesus's teachings. You can almost hear the patient frustration in Jesus' voice when he repeatedly says, "Don't you understand?"

While witnessing the Messiah doesn't quite compare to the more minor occurrence of seeing Spirit's presence in life, people today still get overcome by the shock-and-awe factor when Spirit speaks to them. I, too, went through an evolutionary period in my spirituality to expand my perspective to one that would allow me to believe in infinite possibilities.

After I got over how profound it was to receive these messages, I could focus on their meaning. Receiving Greg's intuitive messages like, "You are so much more than you think," and "I've got more things to show you," reminded me of Jesus' words, "You will see greater things than this" (John 1:50, NLT).

Whether it was a numerical synchronicity, an intuitive message, or a transcendental meditation into another realm, I learned to put my awe on the back burner so as not to miss or distort the intended meaning.

From Possibility to Truth

When we witness a miracle (like the rebirth of a loved one's soul energy), the miracle itself doesn't inspire us to believe. It happened in the material universe and can be scientifically explained. There's no magic in that. The magic of the miracle comes from its contextual meaning, the circumstances surrounding it, and the divine timing it occurred in. Seeing a miracle allows us to accept its *possibility*. Faith from one's heart allows us to accept it as *truth*.

Jesus asked, "Will you never believe in me unless you see miraculous signs and wonders?" — John 4:48, NLT

People accept the news of scientific breakthroughs in quantum physics. But the average person doesn't demand to read the research report of every experiment supporting these claims. It's not needed to accept the information as *truth*. Instead, people use signals like the credibility of the news source, the author's expertise, and the publisher's authority, along with an automatic analysis of whether the claim fits with what they know to be true. In other words, they use **faith** to connect the dots.

You can accept quantum physics breakthroughs on faith because you were taught science in school. Thus, you know enough about it to feel sure in your agreement. If you question your faith, it means there's more exploring for you to do.

The burden of proof isn't on the Divine or Spirit to produce. It's on us to understand ourselves, our world, and Scripture to make sense of things in a way we can jive with. That's what the inner work of a spiritual awakening accomplishes. Choosing to believe opens us up to the universe's infinite possibilities. It heightens our perceptual field and supports humanity's ascension.

The Biofield and the Heart

"Man's perceptions are not bounded by organs of perception; he perceives far more than sense (tho' ever so acute) can discover." —William Blake

If you want to talk about miracles, look no further than the power of the heart—an integral part of the biofield.

People have suspected for millennia that the body contains energy fields. We see it in ancient traditional Chinese medicine with the theory of meridians, which are channels that transmit life force or chi throughout the body. We also see it in the medical community with things like an electrocardiogram (ECG) that measures the electrical field produced by the heart.

The Biofield

The biofield is an invisible energy field that surrounds and interpenetrates all living things. It's responsible for maintaining one's health and well-being. Common energy medicine modalities that work with the biofield include Reiki, Qigong, acupuncture, homeopathy, biofeedback, sound healing, and light therapy.

Your heart, brain, and even your cells have energy fields that coalesce to create your biofield. Much of the information we infer from the world around us is sensed through the biofield. For instance, the auric layer of the biofield enables you to detect the tension in a room.

The latest in biophysics suggests the electromagnetic fields of the body's cells play a role in physical development, tissue repair, and other processes (Rubik 2015). If that's what is happening at the cellular level, imagine what the body's biofield can do on a larger scale!

As humanity continues the ascension journey, new ways to use the biofield to communicate will be unlocked.

The Heart

The heart is a key source of electromagnetic energy. It radiates a toroidal energy field that extends approximately five feet out from your body. Humans are designed to be able to sense this field and infer information through it. This is why the heart is regarded as one of the most powerful tools in one's spiritual arsenal.

The heart is also associated with love, the highest frequency you can produce naturally. Living from a place of love will get you closest to the higher frequency of 5D.

Did you know the heart's electrical amplitude is about sixty times greater than the brain's? The heart's magnetic field is 5,000 times stronger than the brain's and measures several feet away from the body (McCraty, 2023). The heart's energy field allows us to infer information about someone that we can use to navigate our interactions with them. That's where the saying, "knowing the content of one's Heart" comes from. Using this as an information source is much more reliable than relying on a person's word, which is filtered through their ego for them to verbalize. The heart emanates unfiltered energy that can signal a person's intentions, traits, and essence.

Connecting the Heart, Faith, and Twin Flames

In meditation, I often ask my guides and late Twin Flame about God. They're always quick to remind me that abilities like manifestation and telepathy are skills on loan from the Divine; God first demonstrated the ability of manifestation when He created the universe with the power of His word. We manifest things in the 3D because the world is a function of vibration and frequency. It's entangled with higher dimensions like the 5Dand non-physical realms.

To love another person is an exercise of faith. Love asks you to believe in what's in your heart regardless of any doubt or fear you have about the relationship. By living with an open heart, you can transcend above the worldly, egoic things that try to disrupt your faith. Once you do this, things make sense on a whole new level and it's easier to access the frequency of miracles.

Dreams create vision.
Vision creates intention.
Intention creates manifestation.
Manifestation creates reality.

9 Steps to Prepare for a Miracle

1. **Do the inner work.** As with any change, it starts from within. Aligning with the frequency of miracles begins with introspection, shadow work, and exploration at the soul level. Take note of life's lessons. Where have things like mirroring, past trauma, or karmic baggage hindered you? What lessons do you need to learn?

2. **Heal.** Use tools like the Violet Flame to heal past traumas, alchemize old energy that no longer serves you, and remove blockages. This step is critical for living with an open heart.

3. **Set your intention... and commit to it.** Intention-setting is important for achieving any goal, especially a metaphysical one. Unlike setting a goal or a New Year's resolution, setting an intention is a shift in your entire mindset. Everything you do should be on the frequency of what you're trying to attain. Remember, *thoughts become things*.

4. **Listen to your inner voice.** Separate intuition from ego, and learn to value your intuitive guidance as much as you value material guidance. Trust what you're receiving as true no matter what doubts arise. If you're right, you'll gain a miracle. If you're wrong, then OK, you'll at least be in a better position for having practiced faith and gratitude.

5. **Meet your Spirit guides.** Finding out who your Spirit guides are to you will yield essential information about who *you* are and your purpose in life. Your guides are always there to help you and can catalyze the spiritual journey. Meditate and ask them to reveal themselves.

6. **Work with your partner's higher self**. Energy sessions like Reiki healing and meditation allow you to work with your partner's energy even if they've passed away or live halfway across the globe. Bypass the ego and material world distortion, and go straight to their higher self. Remember that you affect them as much as they affect you, so you can help

drive the connection to inspire the personal development you seek.

7. **Be mindful of the world around you.** Signals are always being sent through the spatial universe to us. What synchronicities are you experiencing? What cosmic events are taking place? Everything has a purpose. Everything occurs in divine timing. These things can help derive meaning and give you the confirmation you need.

8. **Fall in love with yourself.** To universally love others, we must universally love ourselves. See yourself the way your Twin Flame, spouse, child or someone who universally loves sees you. Fall in love with yourself like you fall in love with your partner. Cherish yourself the way a divinely beautiful being deserves.

9. **Live each moment like you're already in union.** Live as if you've already achieved what you're hoping for. Doing so sends the universe the signal to manifest it in reality.

Wrapping Up the Inner Work

Doing the inner work formed a deep respect for everything I'd been blessed to experience. The process expanded my understanding of life and death. It released me from grief and delivered me into grace. I was no longer disappointed by my loss and had grown to appreciate Greg in Spirit as much as I loved him in the 3D. My heart overflowed with how grateful I was to know him and feel his Spirit with me for the rest of my days.

I transcended the limits of my shortsighted viewpoint and bridged the gap of my human ability by placing full trust in myself, my guides, and God. I had no desire to change things or force the situation into what *I* wanted. I recognized that my higher self knew what was best for me. Grace, gratitude, and love leveled me up to experience the magic of miracles and brought me one step closer to finding my late Twin Flame.

I committed to the challenge of higher living, ready to receive the incredible things being promised by Spirit. I was being called to bring *everything* into a higher frequency, including how I viewed the struggle-ridden, traumatic, and dark events from my past. These things didn't happen *to* me as a consequence of life's chaotic nature. They happened *for* me along my divine path. The lessons they yielded were now a part *of* me.

Shifting to this perception rendered the damage from my past traumas inert because **low-frequency things like fear, anger, and shame can't exist when you're resonating at a higher state.**

Aligning with the Frequency Miracles

The flow of the universe is meant to be worked with, not resisted. Miracles occur when you flow with the universe and God with pure intentions toward your highest path.

The frequency you're living at determines the frequency of what can exist around you. In this way, you are a co-creator of your reality and the world. Align with the frequency of miracles, and that is what you'll receive.

Though I didn't know exactly how it'd come to be, I now believed Greg's promise that he was "coming back." I had faith that I'd find my Twin Flame again.

The first go-around with Greg wasn't exactly smooth sailing, so there was a level of fear involved in welcoming his return into my life. I could be opening myself up to the hardship and challenges that come with the Twin Flame relationship, like the running, the chasing, and the separation. But I didn't allow those seeds of fear to take hold. Aware that "what you focus on grows," I chose to acknowledge only the beautiful, infinite potential. After all, we can only experience love in its highest form when we're fearless and free.

Letting My Twin Flame Guide Me

The universe gives daily reminders of its infinite possibilities. Like many people experiencing an awakening, I thought I was losing it when I first started seeing all the signs, messages, and synchronicities. I had trouble allowing myself to believe and shrugged it off, believing it was all in my head. When the messages didn't stop coming, it became impossible to ignore that my Twin Flame was intuitively guiding me.

Every day, I'd see something new. I'd capture photos of lens flares that spanned the entire visible spectrum of light. I'd receive messages as small as a funny joke or as profound as statements of wisdom. I'd hear a song on the radio at just the right time to make me smile.

Because of my openness to let my Twin Flame guide me, I grieved in a healthy way and learned to see my loss as an unfortunate blessing. I took advantage of every bit of encouragement offered by these enlightening moments. I felt less stressed and anxious than I had in years. I was in tune with myself and the world around me. I saw how all the pieces fit together, building up to something greater.

Chapter 11

The Universe Confirms a Miracle Is Coming

Spirit never surprises us out of the blue. Signs and signals of life's metaphysical current are always visible if we're open to them. The journey of my Twin Flame's rebirth was no different. In the five or six months it'd take to reach this miracle, the universe seemed to be doing everything it could to send me confirmation—to reinforce my belief that a rebirth was possible.

Greg's energy was strong after he died. So strong that other people noticed his presence. People started messaging me on social media, including family members and friends, and people who'd never even met Greg. They said they felt his presence or that Greg had been on their minds, and they intuitively felt that he wanted me to know that.

It wasn't like this was coming from a psychic or medium who knew what to look for and how to infer messages. These were everyday people. While everyone can read and receive energy, if someone isn't aware of their abilities, it's even more meaningful when they're so impacted by a psychic experience that they feel compelled to reach out and share it.

This was confirmation that the supernatural, metaphysical things I was witnessing weren't just in my head. He was really trying to get my attention.

Carah's Message

On the night of February 10, 2021 (here we go with more numerical synchronicities of ones and twos), nineteen days after Greg died, I was sitting on my porch staring up at the night sky. I'd just gotten off the phone with a friend after a heavy

108

conversation about my grief. I looked at the horizon and noticed that every star in the sky appeared to have a corresponding star that matched it, as if they were paired up and divinely coupled. My big orange cat was outside with me. He interrupted my star-gazing when, out of nowhere, he began meowing and acting strange. It was like he was excited about something. Perhaps he felt something in the energy because, a few moments later, I received a message from my old friend, Carah.

Carah and I hadn't talked in over a decade. She lived halfway across the country and, like me, was undergoing a spiritual awakening. Without wasting time on pleasantries, she started sending me audio clips. She felt a strong energy come through to her and was channeling it. I immediately recognized the energy as Greg's.

Carah was being intuitively guided to deliver messages as they came through. She brought up things that were dead-on about who my Twin Flame was as a person, though she'd never met him. One of the things she mentioned involved the ocean or beach, which related to Greg's "calisurferboy" persona. It was also the scene my guides would take me to in meditation in the coming months. Carah knew nothing about Greg's old AIM username or that Spirit's preferred setting was a beach scene. She didn't have to because this was coming from Spirit. Carah also included something about Leo. My daughter's sun sign is in Leo, but a greater meaning would be revealed later in my journey.

After about ten minutes, the channeling ended. In an instant, I felt my Twin Flame's presence return. I was blown away. It wasn't just me! It wasn't in my head. Everything I was thinking, feeling, and experiencing was credible and real. It was exactly what I needed to remove any doubt that these were mere coincidences. Resolving my doubt unlocked the spiritual floodgates.

Meditation

After Carah's channeling, I had a nagging feeling that Greg wanted to say more, like he was sending me things to get my attention, but I wasn't receiving the entire message. I wondered if Greg was just messing with me by teasing me with all the synchronicities and odd occurrences and would never deliver the full message.

I've mentioned meditating many times before in this book, but it was at this point in the timeline that I tried meditating for the first time. I wasn't expecting it to be significant, let alone for it to last hours. Then again, I didn't know what to expect. I left it open for Greg to show me whatever it was that was so urgent that he had to communicate through Carah.

The next time I felt Greg's energy, I jumped at the opportunity to connect with him. I threw my hands up and said out loud, "You've got something to tell me? OK, fine. Let's go. Tell me."

A Different Kind of Meditation

I moved to a quiet, dark room of my house and lay flat on the floor. I could feel Greg's presence and was excited to see what would happen. Almost immediately after closing my eyes, I began feeling strange sensations all over my body. There was a heaviness in my limbs. A sense of eagerness filled my chest. An anxious energy radiated from my heart space. Tingling sensations moved through my feet and up my legs, going through my entire body. I couldn't believe what I was experiencing just by lying down (and the meditation hadn't even really begun!).

Electric vibrations continued to localize in my body. I felt a warmth near my navel at my sacral chakra. This chakra correlates to one's creative and sexual energy. I was absolutely floored (no pun intended) when all the energy and excitement at my sacral chakra had me sexually stimulated.

I didn't understand how I could feel all that without moving a muscle, with no one else in the room, and with no physical stimulation. I couldn't help but feel like Greg was messing with me.

He loved to tease me and get me all worked up, then bask in the ego boost and physical allure of his accomplishment.

Trying my best to not get distracted by how mind-blowing it was, I tried to release my focus and just feel. I had total mental clarity, but something was different. I wasn't perceiving with my mental mind. I was perceiving through my consciousness. The sensations were then augmented by flashes of light and color—perhaps from my third eye activating.

A mental image of Greg appeared in my mind's eye. I didn't just see him; I *felt* him as if he was lying next to me. I felt pressure on different parts of my body and could feel him touch me. No words were exchanged, but there was no shortage of communication. The experience was chock-full of meaning and messages. Greg was using this opportunity to show what was possible. It was an introduction to using energy to interact.

After spending some time with Greg in the ether and reveling in the power of meditation, I ended the session with a heartfelt "See you later." I didn't want to leave, but I felt things had reached a natural point of conclusion. I also knew I'd need to process everything that had just happened. As soon as I grounded myself back into the 3D and opened my eyes, I wanted to go right back and do it again.

The meditation lasted for an hour and a half. In that time, I wasn't grieving. Greg wasn't gone. It wasn't a dream created by my subconscious. He was right there, closer to me than ever. It was his actual energy that I was detecting and interacting with. The way he came through to me was unique to us, something I could identify as him in any time, space, or method. I knew there was another level of meditation I hadn't broken through to, and was eager to try again to reach it.

Transcendental Meditation

The term *transcendental meditation* was coined by Maharishi Mahesh Yogi in the 1950s. It involves reaching a state of harmony and self-realization by repeating mantras in your mind. When I refer to transcendental meditation, I'm not describing the traditional definition of this term. I literally mean that the meditation session is *transcendental*, in that the experience transcends the physical 3D world and propels you into an otherworldly, nonphysical realm.

While modern science and technology aren't yet able to fully explain this phenomenon, the testimony of others and the similar stories they tell lend credibility to meditation as a tool for connecting to higher realms and dimensions.

Golden Ray Activation

I was lying in bed, unable to sleep from the excitement of the crazy meditation I'd had earlier that day. I was amazed that all of that was possible simply by lying down, closing your eyes, and allowing your brainwaves to adjust and your consciousness to expand. I'd just experienced a whole new world—one where I could see, hear, and even feel my late Twin Flame.

I wanted more of that first session, but I knew it had to be for the right reasons to work. If I attempted to use meditation to be with Greg for self-indulgence or to mask my grief, I wouldn't be able to access that higher state. My lower-frequency motivations would block our communication.

I waited for my intuition to get the invitation to connect the way I had the first time. The hour was getting late. Right as I lay down to go to sleep, the signal came! I felt an intuitive nudge that the energetic circumstances were primed for a higher connection. I closed my eyes to begin the session and was transported to another place.

I found myself sitting on the shoreline of an ocean cove, watching the ocean's waves roll in. I realized I wasn't alone. I looked over to see Greg sitting next to me, gazing out into the sea's abyss. He had darker hair, different from the dirty blond hair I usually pictured him with. I wondered why he was appearing with this darker shade. His white, loose-fitting shirt contrasted the tan of his skin tone. The landscape around us was familiar yet foreign to me. The sand was a lighter color than the beaches we'd been to in real life. The water was a clear shade of blue. The wind blew calmly, and the waves broke in a peaceful, gentle way as they flowed toward us. It wasn't daytime, but the sun wasn't setting yet, either. A beautiful golden light illuminated the beachy scene.

The meditation went on to a second scene. A train zipped by me at high speed. The train was a marvel of sharp engineering, solid craftsmanship, and precise calculation. It symbolized something bigger and stronger than myself—a force that I, alone, couldn't stop or control but was a safe and reliable means of transportation. As I watched as one train car after another went by, I realized what they were carrying: my life.

Each car played out a different moment in my life, as if I was watching the events on a movie screen. Though the train was moving at a super-fast speed, I could recognize the events of my life that each car contained. Before long, I found myself hovering above the train, totally out of my body, with Greg by my side.

This was my chance to ask Greg the pressing questions that were eating at me. With the train moving steadily below us, I asked questions about our relationship. When I asked him questions about the future like, "What am I supposed to do next?" I couldn't make out his answer. Or he didn't answer at all because the point of this experience was to be in the moment. Something significant was going on in the undertow, below the surface of our talk. Like an energy download or activation that would be revealed in divine timing.

After more than an hour, the session came to an end. When I opened my eyes and rejoined the real world, I felt mentally rested and clearheaded, though I was physically exhausted from the intense energy it took to sustain a session of that magnitude for that long.

Next thing I knew, in the pitch blackness of my apartment, I heard my toddler daughter wake up in her room down the hall. The timing was almost too perfect: I had just enough time to become fully grounded in the world again. When I went to check on her, her toy dog, which talks when you press its paw, had activated. It was all the way across the room from her bed, so I know she didn't press it. I didn't know what to make of this and was honestly a little bothered that it involved my daughter (Boundaries, ghosty!).

I put Everly back to sleep and reflected on my meditation experience. There was a golden glow in my visions from a light source I couldn't quite make out. I interpreted the gold lighting as having some kind of significance but couldn't put my finger on what it was. And why the train? Greg might've chosen the visualization of a train to convey his message because it directly related to a past experience when I "chased a train" from Charlotte to Cary, North Carolina. It was such a big endeavor that the parents of a close friend of mine remember me as "the girl who chased the train."

The Train: Your Purpose

Twenty-one months after this meditation (yep, another instance of numerical synchronicity), a vision of the train from the meditation appeared in a dream. It was the final scene in my dreams that night, as though purposely positioned to remember when I awoke.

That morning, I decided to buy a big-ticket piece of art from a local artist. The large canvas painting titled "Reverence" depicted the sun's rays shining through a tree's leaves to create a burst of colorful frequency. The artist painted it after a personal miracle occurred in her life, and she witnessed this beautiful display of nature as confirmation. Something in me knew that if I acted on my intuition, things would open up and support my highest path. Hesitant of the price but determined to trust my inner knowing, I agreed to purchase this work of art that fit me so perfectly.

Later that day, the artist posted about the Vision Train on social media. According to the Vision Train website, "The Vision Train is an interactive art movement linking our visions into a self-manifesting destination of the most inspiring future."

As soon as I saw her post, I reached out to share the vision of the train I'd seen in my dream the night before. I mentioned how it was depicted in a golden light. She gasped and then sent me a photo of a painting by the Vision Train's founder. The painting was of an elaborately decorated, powerful steam engine protruding from the sea's waves like it was being birthed from the water into a golden landscape. The cars of the train were intricately painted and decorated with unique styles from across the world.

At that moment, everything came together: the train in my inaugural meditation, the golden light, and its reappearance in my dream the night before. They were clues from Spirit to help me along my path, confirmation that this was exactly where I was supposed to be.

Trains are where people intersect on their different paths in life. They meet, connect, maybe gain something from their experience or perhaps just relax, then go their separate ways to continue their respective journeys. While the people venture off into what they think is the unknown, the train tells us otherwise. The train has a defined path. It's predetermined by the train tracks, which we can equate to the divine path of God's plan for us. The experiences we have become of higher importance than our destination.

Golden Light

The one thing that kept standing out about these spiritual experiences was the presence of golden light. In spirituality, the gold light or Golden Ray contains the wisdom and illumination necessary for spiritual evolution. For me, the gold light symbolized the Golden Ray Twin Flames, a group of Twin Flames who are responsible for Earth's ascension. Spirit was signaling to me that I am a Gold Ray Twin Flame. Realizing this truth unlocked ancient inner knowledge engraved in my soul so my human self could access it.

Gold Ray Twin Flames

Like your aura, your Twin Flame resonance also has a color. Each color connects with a chakra within the twelve-chakra system and corresponds with the mission you're here to fulfill. The Gold Ray Twin Flame relates to the gold or shimmery multicolored light of the Divine Gateway or Stellar Gateway chakra—the twelfth chakra. It encompasses ascension and oneness with the Divine. When this chakra is unlocked, it's said to wield spiritual knowledge for guiding others to achieve this cosmic connection.

Twin Flames with the Golden Ray have a very serious mission and are responsible for facilitating the ascension of humanity. They're tasked with the heavy lifting of raising up the world for the good of others rather than for the benefit of themselves. The ego does not define who they are, which is seen in how they approach life. Additionally, they possess the Golden Ray's healing abilities and can heal people who are spiritually lost.

Having reached a higher level of spiritual evolution, they've accumulated a good deal of wisdom along the way and use this knowledge to raise the vibration of humanity. While this might seem like a hopeless task to others, Gold Ray Twin Flames feel called to persist in their mission no matter how chaotic the world may seem. In short, Gold Ray Twin Flames play a big role in the rapid spiritual awakening of Earth.

How It Feels to Connect at Higher Levels

The impact of the intensity in my first meditations inspired me to start meditating daily, and this helped me to feel close to Greg. I continued to work with his higher self to close out any unfinished business between us and resolve the things we hadn't had the chance to when he was alive.

Today, the process of raising my body's vibration in meditation helps me tap into the metaphysical web my soul is tied to. I've even met my own soul or higher self in meditation! Raising my frequency allows me to better hear, see, and feel their energy.

First, I get the physical sensation of my body's energy centers (chakras) coming into alignment. If there's a blockage or imbalance, my guides lend me their energy to aid the process. There's a sort of ticklish, light feeling in my eyes. It extends upward in a spiral oscillation through the top of my head at the crown chakra. From there, it's like my spirit is freed from my body and can ascend.

In this state, I can experience my Twin Flame in a way that rivals experiencing him in the physical, material world. My senses are triggered in a way where I can feel the weight of his body resting on mine as if he is next to me. It's wild! This effect isn't a product of the brain. It's not being powered by the principle of "mind over matter," where you can mentally trick your brain into firing synapses to make you believe you're sensing something that isn't there. This situation has another layer—one of metaphysical energy or Spirit.

If we can create this kind of mind-blowing, reality-shattering experience with no external stimuli to trigger us and no physical matter causing it, then the human body-mind-soul combination is truly more powerful than we ever thought.

Psychic Readings, Past Life Regression, and Spirit guides

Shortly after Greg died, I started to feel like this wasn't our first rodeo together. We'd experienced each other's deaths before. To explore this, I did something else I'd never done: I booked a session with a psychic medium.

I found a local metaphysical store that offered readings by qualified practitioners. The only opening they had was almost two weeks away, on Valentine's Day. Coincidentally, that day—February 14, 2021—had significance from Greg's misdated letters written a year earlier. What were the chances?

I went into the reading wearing my best poker face. My inner skeptic wanted to be sure the information the reader channeled was real. I told the psychic nothing about myself other than mentioning that someone close to me had recently died.

The reading started with the psychic confirming the energy she was picking up was from the intended person. She described their appearance as it was coming through in her mind's eye, giving a dead-on description of Greg's facial structure. She asked if he was kind of preppy, which didn't resonate a first, but she quickly added details like a fitted shirt, jeans, and flip-flops. This is exactly how Greg usually appeared to me. I recognized the energy she was channeling. It *was* him.

She said that people in Spirit choose how they appear to us and often present themselves as they looked at the happiest times in their life. This was confirmed for me when she said he was coming through to her with dirty blond hair. Greg's hair is naturally dark brown but was blond when we were together in our early twenties... the romantically blissful part of our Twin Flame journey.

The psychic finished identifying Greg's energy with one last detail: "He's got a red car." I told her that was incorrect. Greg has had cars painted teal, blue, gold, and silver and a black truck. Then, it hit me: Greg's mom recently told me she'd painted his treasured pickup truck in his favorite shade of cherry red in memoriam. He *did* have a red vehicle. I was astounded.

The reader noted that he was coming in very strong, as if he was standing in the room with us. This was similar to the strong energy signature I'd felt in my own experiences with him. I felt the energy coming from the right side of the room but didn't share this out loud. She used her hands to motion to where she detected his energy. It was the exact spot that I'd detected.

We strayed from the topic of Greg for a moment to do a tarot card reading. As she explained the cards to me, Greg interjected. He manifested a physical sensation on her back to get her attention. She relayed his message that if I ever felt something near my upper shoulder, it was his signal to me. She didn't know that the specific spot she referred to had significance. This was "his spot," where he'd give me soft kisses and watch as I reacted to how ticklish it was. Hearing it referenced in the reading hushed my inner skeptic. I had no reason *not* to believe this was real.

I also learned that after Greg died, his Spirit went through a healing process, which is typical for souls who've crossed over. Leading up to the appointment, Greg's energy was inconsistent. Sometimes I felt his fierce love for me. I knew he was devoted to our union. Other times, it felt like he was far away, on the fence about whether he would remain committed to this lifetime with me. Perhaps this was caused by going through the healing process.

"He's been busy," she said. "He's been making his rounds to visit the people in his life." I was in awe. This explained why I would feel his presence come and go, as if he went to be with someone else, like his grieving mother or brothers, to keep them company. When I'd feel his energy depart, my ego couldn't help but feel a bit jealous. I wanted his full attention. I'd have to let this go and learn to have confidence in the special connection we shared, regardless of anyone else.

The reader then added that Greg and I had a long history together. We've played different roles for each other in past lives. This explained the unusual connection I felt to him.

"So, what now?" I asked.

"He'll act as a guide to you. He's got some things he wants to show you." What a mysterious, intriguing way to end a reading!

Learning About Twin Flames

Around the time of the reading, a long-lost best friend came back into my life. The timing of her reentry was hard to ignore, especially considering she was the one who introduced me to the idea that Greg and I were Twin Flames. It's as if my friend came into my life with divine timing to unlock this path for me.

Over the next few weeks, I integrated the information from my psychic reading session but struggled to understand it in the context of Twin Flames. Additionally, the energetic occurrences I was experiencing showed no sign of stopping. I needed to understand why these things were happening. I reached back out to the reader for advice. She replied with this beautiful piece of wisdom:

"Often, romantic relationships are the ones we learn from the most—especially when it comes to Twin Flames. Because you are two of the same soul, there is that *magnetism*. Think of it like magnets—if one component is missing from what makes a magnet stick, it will force the other away. If there is unresolved energy on either side of Twin Flames, it makes it hard to stick. Now that your Twin is on the other side, he's able to act as a guide. Since he is part of your soul, in a weird way, his voice *is* your own consciousness. Keep listening to that voice because he's always going to want the best for your journey, no matter what."

That night, I journaled about what the reader had told me:

I'm being promised a miracle. I'm being asked to completely let go of what was and open up to something that I can't wrap my head around yet. I don't see how it would be possible for me to not have the opportunity to finish out whatever the purpose for all of this is. I know I won't get to finish the journey with who I once knew. But it will be his same heart... one that I'd know anywhere. If there's one thing Greg did, he strived to break the limits of the word "impossible."

Past-Life Regression

The idea that Greg and I shared past lives piqued my interest. If I was going to understand this part of our history, I needed more information. I searched online for a past-life regressionist and found Irina Nola, who just so happened to offer Twin Flame regression sessions. I was impressed by her credentials, which included a formal BA degree in psychology and certifications in hypnotherapy, past-life regression therapy, and Quantum Healing Hypnosis Technique (QHHT) from Dolores Cannon's QHHT Academy.

I emailed her to schedule a Twin Flame regression, which regresses to the origin point of two souls—the moment the soul meets their counterpart for the first time. This can yield insight into why a person feels connected to their partner and what they're here to accomplish in this life. I included info about Greg's recent passing in my message. But there was a problem: Irina wouldn't work with me while I was grieving.

Irina responded to my request and explained:

"It's not a good time to do any regression hypnosis when you are grieving. The energy is low, and it makes it impossible to access fifth-dimensional reality, which is necessary to read Akashic records and contact the guides."

I appreciated the discernment for her client's well-being. But Greg's death hadn't sent me into a depressive state of grief. It *energized* me. I was able to access the 5D and connect at this level but needed help exploring this heightened connection. After a few email exchanges, Irina saw this and agreed to do the regression.

The Seed Point

My session with Irina covered things like witnessing the birth of my and Greg's spirits from the same monad of soul energy. After learning that Greg and I share monadic soul energy, I was taken to a past life in the Preclassic period (2,000 BCE–250 CE). We lived in a Mesoamerican civilization like the Maya. We were deeply in love and had the same magnetic connection as we have in this life.

Society valued fertility. Procreation was extremely important. Women who could produce children were married off and played an active role in their households and community. They could practice rituals that women of lower statuses could not. After failed attempts to become pregnant, I felt the soul-crushing heartache of being unable to bear a child.

Since I was unable to reproduce, Greg took a concubine, as per local custom. I spent my remaining lifetime watching my lover with another woman. Building a family. Enjoying the privileges that came with it. Privileges I wasn't afforded as a single, barren woman. I endured decades of heart-stabbing pain.

Every time our paths crossed in that small village, the pain went deeper and deeper. It instilled feelings of betrayal, abandonment, and pain—feelings I recognized from my current lifetime. I wondered how much of this strife was carried over into this lifetime and projected onto situations to create unnecessary struggle between us. The only way I could manage the pain and not feel like part of me was ripped out was to put him out of my mind. He was dead to me. This is a parallel to my experience in

present-day life and eerily similar to how I coped during the separation period.

This past life was the **seed point,** the first time we fell victim
to the illusion of separation of ourselves from our monadic soul
counterpart. It was the first time we felt the pain of being separated from the person we knew to be part of ourselves. No matter
how badly we wanted to be together, the social customs of that
time forbid our union.

Healing Across Timelines

Things like this come to our attention so we can heal from
them. More than a year and a half after my regression session,
that's exactly what I did. Finding the origin or seed point helped
me see through the illusion of separation and heal millennia of
pain. (It's possible to heal the burdensome pain and trauma
you've accumulated across time. You're not powerless against
the impact of past, present, or future events.)

On November 20, 2022 (notice the ones and twos in the date
again), I revisited this seed point in meditation to heal it once and
for all. With the aid of my guides and my Twin Flame's higher self
brought to mind, I visualized Greg and me. We went through a
process to accept what was. We alchemized the negativity, baggage, and things that didn't serve us and used this to catalyze
our healing. No longer weighed down by these things, we focused
our energy on *all* lifetimes we're connected to.

This healing love was sent out to all our past and future incarnations—the fragments of our souls had been suspended in
time, waiting for us to take this action. This act of healing resolved the fragments and brought them to a functional state to
rejoin with our higher selves in harmony. In a sense, it made us
whole again.

Manifesting through Journaling

I journaled about my experiences, like the past-life regression and synchronicities, to document the journey. Journaling doubled as a manifestation tool. After all, if the universe could be created with God's Word, surely I could co-create my path in my own life with my words.

I wrote letters to my future self, embodying the energy of having found my late Twin Flame again. I acted like my miracle was already here and sent this out into the universe to be heard.

I wrote letters to Greg, thanking him for the lessons he taught me and the love he showed me. I attempted to cope with how I'd lost him to an overdose and understand the pain he was in. I wanted to see the world through his eyes and appreciate who he was underneath the upsets, arguments, and issues we'd had over the years. I worked through these things to the point where all that was left was my pure love for him.

Automatic writing, where you enter a meditative state and write whatever flows through you, also proved to be fruitful and offered inspiring messages like:

- You are never alone. Your guides are always with you, guiding you to your highest purpose.

- Your past lives reveal deep soul wisdom for you to utilize in your current incarnation.

- Demonstrate this wisdom through your actions, not just your words.

- This time is meant for you to understand, value, and cherish something as great as what you're about to receive so that you can fully appreciate it.

- God is working to bring you what you deserve.

- When you're aligned with Spirit's will, miracles are possible.

Communication Through Letters

I could also find evidence in Greg's old letters to me to confirm the legitimacy of all the wild, spiritual things I was experiencing. One of the tools he used to manage his emotions was writing. We'd be sitting in the same room together, and he'd be scribbling away in his notebook, writing letters to gather his thoughts and communicate his feelings. After he passed, these letters became priceless. They were a window into his soul, a way to understand his view of the world.

In one of his writings, Greg recounts the intense bond we share. He talks about how our connection is set apart from the connection we have with anyone else. Though we didn't know the correct terminology for it then, Greg knew in his heart that we were Twin Flames. What's more, he writes, **"the universe always puts us back together. *Always.*"** His conviction in this statement is riveting, as is how it fits with the intrinsic notion that he will return to me. Here's an excerpt from his letter:

> We have the most incredibly strong and intense bond/connection that other people only wish they could have with someone. We have a love, passion and attraction for each other that we would never be able to have with anyone else in a hundred years. Even if we wanted to try and get away from each other, the universe always puts us back together. Always.

Valentine's Day Synchronicity

It was surprising when I came across not one, but three letters erroneously postdated for a date that was *after* he died. They were post-dated for February 14, 2021—one year in the future.

One of these three documents wasn't just a letter; it was his Valentine's Day gift to me: a beautifully crafted declaration of his love for me, handwritten in cursive on heavy paper stock. Though the other two postdated letters could be explained away as him writing too quickly or being distracted, Greg gave this one special attention. He crafted it with care and precision. I couldn't ignore this as a mistake. It was as if his soul knew what was coming and caused him to have a subconscious slip of the pen and date his letters for a time when he'd have my full attention in grief.

Sure enough, when February 14, 2021, rolled around, it proved to be an important day for our Twin Flame journey. In the previous section, the only opening the psychic reader had available was on this day, even though I booked it three weeks in advance. The postdated letters were true synchronicities. They help prove the metaphysical phenomenon of soul connections.

Returned Mail in Divine Timing

On April 9, I received something that was even harder to explain away as an oversight or a mistake: a returned letter in the US Mail. Seeing as how I'd mailed it to Greg in December of the year before, April was an abnormal length of time for it to be returned. I recalled how excited I was to mail it to him, not knowing he wouldn't be on this Earth to receive it. The returned letter arrived at the perfect time to refuel my faith in the universe's connected nature and remind me that everything happens in divine timing.

Chapter 12

Synchronicity of Numbers and Other Signs

One of the first things people notice in a spiritual awakening is the synchronicity of numbers. These can be dates and times, but also any number that appears throughout the day, like the total at the gas pump or data in a spreadsheet at work. Skeptics might say, "You can find *any* number if you look for it!" What's special about numerical synchronicities is that you don't go looking for them. These signs from Spirit find you.

Greg's death prompted me to start seeing the number 444 everywhere, along with the numerical synchronicities of ones and twos. I saw this number at the gas pump and on license plates, mobile phone games, makeup labels, prices, school bus numbers, and street addresses. After more than twenty-four months of seeing 444 at least twice a day (and thinking I was going nuts for seeing it so often), I knew that when I saw this number, my late love was safe, healed, and keeping the promise he made to me during his visit to the Earthly plane.

Meaning of 444

The angel number 444 is a sign of protection and encouragement that you're on the right path. It includes the number 4, the number of the self, hard work, responsibility, and trust, and amplifies it by repeating it three times.

The number 444 recognizes your progress and the effort it took to get there. It reminds you to continue putting in the strength and energy to achieve your purpose. It symbolizes the end of one phase of life and the beginning of another and assures you that you're never alone. You're being guided and embraced with the mystical positive vibrations sent your way.

Dates, Times, and Birthdays

Dates and times are known for being easy indicators of synchronicity and can be viewed as signals of confirmation from the universe.

Greg died on the morning of January 22, 2021. In numerology, this date reduces to 10, a number that signifies the completion of a cycle and the new beginning of the next. It's also the number of enlightenment and spiritual awakening.

Around 10:22 a.m. on the day of Greg's death, the strangest feeling overcame me. It was so strong, it stopped me in my tracks as I was walking along a nature trail. The sensation I felt was from his energy shifting from the physical plane to the spiritual one.

A year before his death, on January 1, 2020, at 10:22 a.m., Greg had an NDE. I called 911, and he was resuscitated. The date reduces to 5, which is associated with trials and challenges (talk about a challenge!).

It's interesting to note the numerals 1 and 2 in these dates and times, which seems to be the pattern for significant events in this journey. It suggests that the events are connected.

Synchronicities can also be found in our zodiac sun signs and birthdates. Greg was Aquarius, and I am Pisces. Aquarius is the water bearer, an air sign that holds the world's cup of water (water symbolizes life or emotion). Pisces, a water sign symbolized by two fish swimming in opposite directions and forever tethered by an unbreakable cord, connects the physical and metaphysical halves of life. Aquarius bears the water, and Pisces is that water.

Other interesting things about our birthdays include:

- We were born **1** year and **20** days apart. (Yep... more ones and twos!)
- His birthday, February 6, and my birthday, February 26, both contain **2** and **6**.
- His full birthdate reduces to **6**, the number of love (6 is The Lovers card in Tarot, traditionally called The Choice card). My birthdate equals **10**, a number that encompasses all the events, experiences, and lessons of a cycle, with 1 as the number of new beginnings and 0 as the infinite nature of eternity.

No single modality can prove (or disprove) the theory of connection and rebirth. It's not the numerology of a specific date or a singular zodiac placement that creates meaning. Meaning is derived from the holistic picture of how each piece fits together in the comprehensive story of one's life.

Sequential Numbers

The shift in patterns can hold just as much meaning as the synchronicities themselves. As the journey progressed, I started to see consecutive number patterns. This differed from the repeating synchronicities like 11:11, 2:22, 3:33, and so on. For instance, I'd see numbers like:

- 12:34
- 1:23
- 4:56
- $78.90

The sequential nature of the numbers was a reminder that I was making progress, growing and developing in the right direction—the direction of a miracle.

Other Signs

There were too many other signs to count. For instance, one day, a song by a band I'd never heard before came on my playlist. The lyrics told me to look at the sky because the person in the song was still present and would be alive next year. That's a pretty direct message!

That same day, I witnessed a heart cloud in the sky, numerical synchronicities such as 12:21 p.m. and $4.44, and a "Heaven & Earth Landscaping" company truck that drove by while a song about "heaven on Earth" played on the radio.

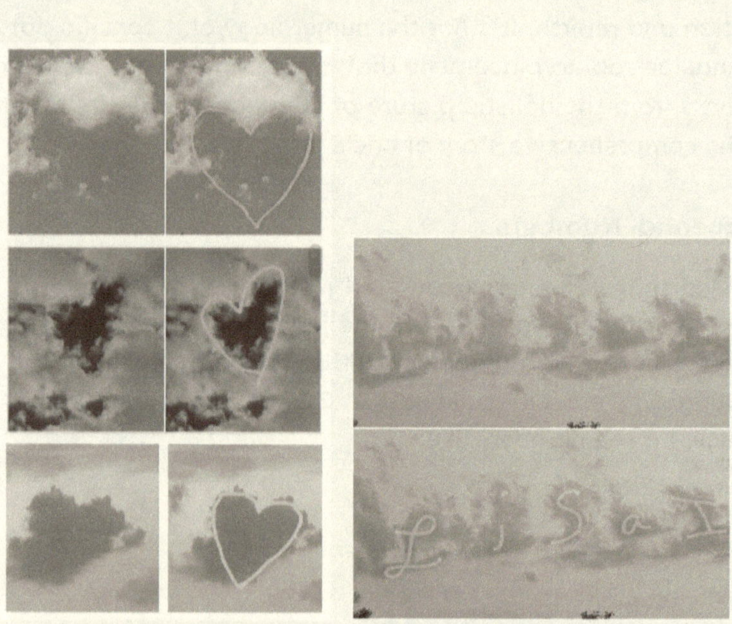

Heart shapes (left) and my name (right) in the clouds.

On another occasion, the song "Amber" by 311 came on my music streaming app for the first time. Greg was into bands like 311 and Incubus, and the timeframe during which this song originated aligned with my time with him. Later that day, I learned that his mom had to sell something precious to their family and had put down one of Greg's favorite German shepherds. The circumstances surrounding hearing this song randomly play were too perfect to be a coincidence.

Here's a note from my journal to Greg on February 12, 2021 (Do I even need to point out the ones and twos?):

>*You continue to send me songs. I am so grateful that you're sharing your journey with me—letting me feel what you do, even if it's on the smallest scale in comparison. That is all I ever wanted: For you to resolve the pain that caused you constant struggle. Have confidence in YOU.*

>*Thank you for allowing me to feel you on the level I do. Thank you for holding up the mirror. Thank you for showing me the self-love that I had lost. Thank you for never losing hope in me. Even if you couldn't uphold the hope 100%, I will keep it burning for the both of us, Love.*

Other signs I've encountered include:

- Angel wings appearing in lens flares of fluorescent lights
- Dragonflies and other animals with significant Spirit meanings, like rabbits and hawks
- Roses, Greg's favorite flower
- Messages in the clouds like my name written in cursive

Light and Lens Flares

Light is something that continues to mystify scientists and spiritualists alike. Some people believe that Spirit can deliver "light codes" to us or activate them within our DNA. Energy can also be transferred through light to deliver messages or energy downloads. Light is a powerful healing tool through which we can receive healing. I witnessed this in the form of lens flares.

Sometimes, it's simply the light refracting, but other times, Greg's energy came in clearly. The lens flares in photos were exponentially more vibrant and intricate. I couldn't force this. It only worked when I felt the energy in the air.

I'd get an intuitive nudge to get out my camera, and I could almost hear the words "point and shoot" in my mind. Or the sun would glimmer like it was trying to get my attention. When the energy was high enough, I could see these beautiful flares in person without the aid of a camera. This is evidence that as our frequency increases and we move upward along the ascension path, our senses expand.

Ghostly Things

I hesitate to include this section because I don't want to focus on low-vibrational things, but it's important to the integrity of the story that I include the worldly, "ghostly" encounters.

Paranormal activity is considered to be low vibrational, while things in Spirit are high vibrational. For a soul to make its presence known in the physical realm, its resonance must be low enough to materialize in the 3D and affect our world. Your loved one's soul doesn't need to turn your life into a scene from *The Shining* to connect with you. However, it's common for the soul energy of a recently deceased person to meddle in paranormal activity just as a starting point to get our attention. This is what I experienced with Greg.

It started small, with random things like realizing the interior light in the backseat of my car was on while I was driving. There was no way for me to turn the light on without manually pushing the button from the backseat. I pulled the car over on the side of the road to take a picture for documentation because I'd been witnessing many small things like this around that time. This occurred the day after my birthday—and twenty-one days after what would've been Greg's thirty-fourth birthday (did you catch the 21?).

From my driver's seat, I turned toward the back of the car to snap a picture and spotted a deer standing right behind my car! The deer was calm and peaceful. It acted as if my multi-ton vehicle with bright-red brake lights was totally normal for it to graze next to. It wasn't spooked or concerned with me at all. While the unexplained rear interior light originally got my attention, the coincidence of the deer convinced me this was a moment of connection.

Years before this, Greg was driving my car on a country road. I was in the passenger seat, and our mutual friend was in the back. I saw a deer on the shoulder of the road up ahead, and asked Greg to slow down. Since it was standing still, he ignored my request and maintained speed. Sure enough, the deer jumped out at the last minute and was struck by my vehicle. We all looked back and saw it lying in the road. We figured it must've died since we hit it going forty-five miles per hour. But on the ride back, the deer's carcass was nowhere to be found. This event turned the subject of deer into a running joke between Greg and me.

Deer are known as totem animals and among the noblest creatures in spirituality. With quiet grace, they move confidently through even the most difficult of times with an understanding that each experience presents a lesson or opportunity. People who feel drawn to deer are said to have special insight into life's deepest truths and understand the immeasurable impact of those who help them grow and evolve. If that isn't the perfect representation of this journey, I don't know what is.

The odd things I experienced weren't causal effects of a chaotic, random universe. They were purposeful and divinely driven. The rear interior light of my vehicle, that was mysteriously turned on caused me to pull over, put me in the right place at the right time to notice the deer and inspire me to take a closer look at the context and symbolism.

Other paranormal activities include the time my daughter and I were watching TV in the living room when suddenly, a sleeve of crackers ejected from out of its box in the pantry closet and onto the kitchen floor. It hit the ground with such force and distance, it looked like it had been thrown. I tried re-creating the scene to see if the crackers might've accidentally been dislodged from the vibrations that traveled through the floor and walls. Even when intentionally positioning them and inching them to the edge of the shelf so they'd fall, I couldn't re-create it. Paired with the synchronicities from that day and other intuitive phenomena, I had no choice but to accept this as an "otherworldly" occurrence.

When I turned inward to use my inner senses rather than looking to events in the material world to define reality, the paranormal instances stopped. My late Twin Flame, my guides, and the universe no longer needed to use low-vibrational methods to get my attention. They could reach me on a higher level.

Messages through Technology

The auto-suggest feature on my mobile phone also exhibited "ghost in the machine" behavior. Greg's name appeared in the auto-suggested words on my text messaging app at odd times. Phones operate with an algorithm to suggest the next best word according to natural language processing. So, if the last word in my sentence was "pickle," and my phone thinks the next logical word is "Greg," that's something to take notice of. Whenever his name came up, I'd pay extra attention to what was going on around me that day—the circumstances, the energy, how I was feeling, and what Spirit might be trying to tell me.

Sometimes I'd catch it in time to select Greg's name and let the text app craft a message using the auto-suggested words. Some of the phrases I got in moments where my heart was telling me that Greg may be trying to get through included:

- *It will be hard to stick with it and to make this work for the both of us. Know that he is near and I will keep you posted anything about me.*

- *He's been busy with the new connection because you have unfinished business in the world.*

- *It wasn't time yet for me to try to remain in the light with you.*

- *We are so damn alike and I am so lucky to have you forever. I hope you like it **when I return to you** much more precious.*

These auto-suggest messages always occurred during a period of high energy, such as the last full moon of 2022—a full moon in Gemini during the Mars retrograde. This was a turbulent time for Twin Flames and other soul connections alike. Around this time, I received another message via this auto-suggest method:

> *Greg was using the same email as the Oversoul and the other one was on the same time period* 😂 *I had to move in with the light* 😂 *to get the best of me and I hope you understand that this is not the way to go about it but* **I will try to find a way to survive and come back from the death.**

This message occurred in the middle of a text conversation with my grandmother about my sister—a situation that had nothing to do with Greg. It didn't make sense that my phone would suggest his name, so when I saw it, I ran with it to see what he had to say.

At the time, I was revising the section of this book that deals with the soul and Oversoul. My phone wasn't connected to my computer, where my manuscript file lived, so there was no way for it to pick up on that and include those themes. I also couldn't help but notice the date: November 30, 2022 (11/30/22). Ones, twos, and a three. Consecutive numbers that symbolize a forward-moving path in numerology.

Electronics: The Flickering Screen

In the first month or so after Greg died, my phone screen would flicker on and off randomly and inconsistently. Bouts of it were so intense, it rendered my phone unusable. After I got over the initial frustration of the malfunction, I realized the screen was acting up at strange times—times of high emotion or energy.

At one point, the screen flickered in a pattern as if it was trying to signal something, like the light of the screen was being used to communicate. I wondered, if I knew morse code, if the blinks would translate to anything?

The behavior of the flickering seemed to be affected by my consciousness. For kicks, I decided to experiment with it. When the screen would begin to flicker uncontrollably, I'd manage my reaction and ensure my physical and emotional signals were calm and collected. I didn't want to "reward" this type of phenomena by giving it a reaction. When I acted like I didn't notice it, the screen's blinking grew more rapid and frequent. It was as if someone was playing with it and trying to attract my attention.

There was no logical explanation for it. The phone wasn't broken or in bad shape. And there definitely wasn't any explanation for the flickering to change behavior in my consciousness experiments.

I surrendered to the idea that this might actually be an *energetic* phenomenon and not a technological one. I interpreted the flickering as a sign to stop and see what my Twin Flame and guides had to say. As soon as I started meditating regularly and listening to Spirit's messages, the phone screen stopped malfunctioning. The issue magically resolved.

Dreams

Before Greg's death, I'd only had a handful of dreams about him. After he died, he appeared in a countless number of dreams. In some of them, I could tell that I was envisioning my subconscious projection of him. In others, I knew with every fiber of my being that it was his soul energy visiting me. There was a distinct difference between the dreams cast by my subconscious, where I was projecting the memory of Greg into the dreamworld, and the dreams that extended into the astral plane and I was experiencing his live presence. Dreaming had now become an energetic tool to connect with the nonphysical world.

It wasn't just *my* dreams. My sister reached out to me in the week following Greg's death. The tone of her voice and the way she spoke indicated she'd had a powerful experience that startled her. She said she had a dream of Greg being cremated. In her dream, she saw him in the fiery chamber and was overwhelmed with a scary feeling that he wasn't fully detached from his body yet. She feared that his soul was conscious of the severe temperatures that his body was subjected to. It shook her up, but I wasn't sure what to make of the dream at the time.

A few days later, Greg's mom told me she'd decided to have him cremated. My sister had no way of knowing that information. It made me wonder if her dream was really a premonition.

Your loved ones who've passed away are likely reaching out through your friends and family. Their messages may be as subtle as an intuitive thought or as distinct as a vivid dream.

Astral Travel

The closer I got to my Twin Flame's rebirth, the more my experiences in meditation evolved.

Less than two months before I'd meet my "new" rebirthed Twin Flame, I heard a high-pitched noise. It sounded like tinnitus, but it came from something other than my ear. I checked for anything electronic around me that could be making the sound, but there was nothing. The sound was *energetic*. It was my sense of hearing's interpretation of a high-resonating metaphysical frequency. Earlier in the day, I had an intuitive sense that my guides were waiting to give me a message. The high-pitched sound was my cue to lie down in a dark, quiet room and meditate to see what they had to say.

When I closed my eyes and drifted off, my closed-eye visuals were extremely active. My guide mentioned something about astral projection and that I could now perform this type of travel. He then advised me to remove the crystals and gems that I had placed overtop of the chakra points on my body, saying they were holding my Spirit back from being able to freely leave the physical world and commune at higher levels.

Once I removed the stones, I closed my eyes again and saw visions of my arms and hands illuminated by a translucent bluish-purple light. This was my astral body. It was moving independently of my physical body. I saw my astral self ascend upward, where Greg was waiting for me. I felt interesting sensations, like I was floating. Even the visuals became more "buoyant," bobbing back and forth. I felt shocks of energy buzz between my ears, within my feet, between my eyes, and more. Each lasting for a fraction of a second and accompanied by a piercing energetic sound as it occurred.

Images flashed rapidly behind my eyelids, appearing on a big 360-degree screen all around me. I was witnessing past, present, and future clips of my life. It was then that I heard my main guide tell me, "You are ready for the next stage of your rebirth," and that my Spirit team was "fine-tuning" my body to prepare it for what was coming.

Chapter 13

The Rebirth of My Twin Flame

The universe was singing a song of assurance with its synchronicities and messages. It was time to decide whether to heed its call to actualize my miracle and receive what I'd been promised or settle within my safe little bubble, rejecting whatever unknown adventure fate had in store for me. It was time to set the intention.

I set the intention to fully—and I mean fully—trust the universe with no reservations, doubts, or ego holding me back. I made this declaration in my journal:

I set the intention to follow my soul's deepest inner knowledge. I trust the universe to support me in finding my Twin Flame here in the now. I have faith in the Divine to grant me this love in the timing that I am ready for. I am grateful for any guidance that may be revealed to me to achieve this. I pray that my Twin Flame be lifted by the love that I hold in my heart for them, and that we both live in its freest, most authentic forms. So be it, and so it is.

Upon writing this, I heard Greg call out to me, **"I'm coming back."** His message came through to me as clear as day.

In that evening's meditation, my soul family surrounded Greg and me in a circle of celebration, rejoicing in our accomplishment of overcoming the limitations and burdens of this life and choosing love.

My "New" Twin Flame Enters

Just two weeks after I set my intention, the new person I'd been promised entered my life. They came crashing into my world with no logical rhyme or reason that anyone could make sense of. I, however, knew what I was bearing witness to... my miracle in the making.

I logged into social media one day and saw I had a friend request from a man named John. When his profile appeared in my friend requests, it didn't catch my eye or jump out to me. But I didn't detect any red flags from him, and, surprised at myself for not having deleted the request already, I went ahead and accepted. This is bizarre in itself, as I usually decline friend requests I receive from random men.

What's even stranger is how I appeared on his radar to begin with. We shared two mutual friends: Dustin, who was Greg's friend from a program he was in before he died, and Marjorie, who was my best friend's ex-girlfriend. While these two people were indirectly connected to me by very important people in my life, I'd later learn that John had no real connection to them. This made it even weirder that this combination of people, and only the two of them, were our overlap.

So, what was it that brought us together? How did Facebook put us in the other's line of sight? We weren't searching for the other. We weren't even actively trying to find love. We didn't live in the same metro area, so Facebook didn't serve my profile to him based on physical distance. I'd soon figure out that this was of divine guidance. But before I could meet John, there were a few more steps to prepare for my Twin Flame's reentry.

The Stepping-Stone

The universe foreshadowed John's arrival by throwing a similar situation at me. On March 12, 2021, right at 12:00 a.m. (you guessed it... the ones and twos again!), I felt the energy change.

It suddenly felt like my Twin Flame was far away, like noise was disrupting our connection and making it difficult to pick up on. I had a moment of panic, unnerved by the feeling of being so distant from Greg's connection. Through an intuitive conversation, I checked in with Greg for answers.

"Your signal is weak. You feel so far away. What's going on?" I asked.

"You know what's going on." He responded with surety. Deep down, I already had the answers. I needed assurance to soothe my doubts.

"So, I'll see you again?"

"Yes, Baby, you will see me again," he assured me. **"I'm coming."**

The next thing I knew, I heard my phone go *ding* as a Facebook notification came through. I opened the app to find a profile that caught my attention. Immediately, I felt Greg's energy return and our connection restore.

The Facebook profile was for a person named Josh—the same name as my best friend (Marjorie's ex). The synchronicities in his profile information were staggering. He listed dates in his profile that were significant to me like my sister's birthday, my best friend's birthday, the New Year's Day that Greg almost died, and the date of my thirteenth birthday party, which I consider to be what set me on the path to meet Greg.

I reached out to Josh, and we hung out a few times. While nothing lasting came from it, these experiences formed a necessary precursor for what would come next. If I hadn't accepted the universe's invitation to explore that first person that'd been dropped into my lap the night of the energy shift in March, I wouldn't be able to fully detect the important things needed in my journey with my "new" Twin Flame, John.

Meeting Josh was a practice run to learn how to manage my faith and trust in the unknown to align with my life path and to show me it was possible to find someone with Greg's soul energy.

A Final Lesson of Self-Love

In a final meditation before meeting my "new" Twin Flame, Greg dropped a bomb of truth that changed my entire mindset.

He said, **"If only you could see yourself the way that I see you."**

Imagine that for a moment. What if you saw yourself from the perception of your spouse, partner, or a family member who loved you universally (unconditionally)?

Loving oneself universally is easier said than done, but I tried to follow this advice by writing an affirmation:

I love myself as much as my significant other loves me. With as much tenacity, intensity, trust, respect, and admiration—that "I'd do anything for you" mentality. I am worthy and deserving of my love and express it with grace and gentleness.

Meeting John, My "New" Twin Flame

I met John on July 28, 2021. This particular week in July holds historical significance. It's the week that my relationship with Greg was founded back in 2008. It's also the week of my (former) wedding anniversary in 2015. John and I'd been talking online for about a week or so. To welcome whatever life had to throw at me with open arms, I left my comfort zone and said a big *YES* to the universe's offer to meet him.

We met up for drinks at a local watering hole—the same place that Greg and I frequented in our younger years. Greg later held a job there. It was right next to the Cary, NC, Amtrak station, too, which brought back memories of my infamous train chase.

Despite these memories, I tried to approach things with a blank slate. I didn't want to project my desires or expectations onto things. I wanted to wait for evidence to reveal itself before I blindly believed that this new person was somehow related to my late Twin Flame.

Upon arriving at the bar/restaurant/arcade, I was nervous. For the first time in ages, butterflies were fluttering in my stomach. I parked my car and saw how lively it was through the front windows as I approached. I entered the double doors and lifted my eyes to the seating section as if my heart knew where to look, and I saw *him*. His physical appearance exceeded my expectations but somehow felt just right. It excited and electrified me. I thought, "Wow, I was not expecting that! OK, yeah, let's do this."

I took my seat next to him. It was loud from other patrons playing arcade games, pool, and watching the sports game. There was some initial awkwardness between us, but also calmness and confidence. We got our drinks and played a round of air hockey to break the ice. Once the initial jitters wore off, we retreated to the outdoor patio to talk.

Through our conversation that night, we learned that we shared a connection to a place I once worked at. He was in a serious relationship with one of my coworkers there, years ago. She had recently passed away after enduring months of struggle and hardship from overdose complications that wore her down and dimmed the light in her soul. It was a painful yet familiar tale. I shared that I, too, had lost someone earlier that year. The pain from our stories didn't trigger a trauma bond. Instead, it created a sense of understanding between us—a level playing field for us to build upon.

When the bar closed, I invited him over to my place. I must point out the insanity of this and how out of character this was for me. I was a young, petite female who lived alone (my daughter was at her dad's for the weekend). Inviting a total stranger back to my place is a risk that I usually never take.

We arrived at my house and our conversation continued into the early morning hours. After a productive first date, I decided to hit the hay. Like a gentleman, John opted to go back to his house to sleep, which was admirable since he lived over an hour away.

We left the night with an eager excitement, but also in shock of how well everything went. Neither of us had expected anything to come of what was supposed to be a casual night out. John and I stayed in touch over the next ten days. It didn't take long to conclude that he was the miracle I'd been promised.

The Connection

With every message, interaction, and synchronicity after meeting John, the universe was yelling at me, "Hey, this is it!"

Countless things confirmed this was the promise fulfilled, but the biggest confirmation was the connection itself. The connection with John resonated with the same energy as my connection with Greg. We had an immediate bond, like we'd known each other in another life and were picking up right where we'd left off.

Energetic Connection

You know how when you hug your significant other versus when you hug your mother or father, it just feels different? Imagine feeling that type of difference, but with an energetic soul connection rather than a physical sensation.

Your connection with someone has its own energy signature that's different from any other connection you have. Like an energy blueprint.

Soul-level connections resonate at a frequency that cuts through all the noise of life. You can always tap into this frequency and *feel* your connection to someone.

Confirming the Rebirth (I found you!)

On August 6, 2021, I accepted that John was the one I was waiting for. It had only been five or six months since Greg's death and mere weeks since I set the intention to accept what the universe had in store.

I journaled:

It's the same energy. The same connection. The same touch and desire. This time, I am ready for things to be brought out in me without fear or doubt holding me back. I'm ready to love and be loved. Thank you, God. Thank you, Spirit guides. Thank you, Love.

This was during the Lion's Gate Portal, a cosmic event where the Earth comes into alignment with the sun in Leo, the Sirius star, and the constellation of Orion's Belt. Lion's Gate approaches its peak on August 8 (8/8) and is said to be an ideal time for one to fulfill their dreams.

Carah's message from the day of my first meditation referenced Leo. John was a Leo sun sign, which is represented by a lion. The symbolism of the lion depicts inner strength, nobility, and valor. Her message about Leo also referenced the timing of my miracle occurring during the Lion's Gate Portal. Everything was connecting.

The milestone of finding John brought a new level of clarity. The timing of things made sense, and life was flowing in perfect harmony. The world wasn't chaotic and uncontrollable. It was sequenced, connected, and full of embeddings to manage life. I had the power to co-create the reality of my dreams.

Chapter 14

Reactivating the Twin Flame Connection

My relationship with John was like being reunited with a long-lost lover. It needed no building, no growing, or nurturing. According to my guides, the person who'd enter my life would be ready to pick up where Greg and I left off. They weren't kidding! There was no "falling in love" stage of the relationship. John and I didn't need to fall in love because we were already in love. Our love for one another was already there, waiting to be activated.

I meditated to verify that John was the person my guides had described. This is what I received from his higher self:

"I am going to fulfill all the promises that [Greg] made to you," he said.

"But who are you to me? Are you part of my soul family? Do you share Greg's higher self?" I asked.

"You know me. You know who I am. We've lived many times before. Remember, baby..."

This answer didn't reveal any actual information about his soul's relationship to me, but the energy exchanged in that moment made it clear that he was closely knit into the fabric of my soul family. I found comfort in this familiarity.

"I am here to help you fulfill your mission," he continued. "I will stand by your side as your doting partner, encouraging you and supporting you in all that you do."

Wow. Way to make a girl swoon!

"Help me in this process," he added. "Everything has already been healed [for my incarnation to follow this path], but I need you to guide me to it."

He was referring to the karmic work that many of us set out to do. My guides told me my partner would be energetically ready for the journey, and John's own testimony (or rather, his higher self's testimony) confirmed it.

With confirmation that I was safely in the hands of my guides and the universe, I breathed a sigh of relief. John and I were free to maximize the full potential of the Twin Flame connection.

An Ocean of Renewal: The Beach Trip

John and I had been dating for about a month when I found a rare availability at a quaint beach house. The property was usually fully booked, so when an opening popped up for the exact days I could take off work, I took it as being "meant to be." We ventured down to Atlantic Beach and met our host, a self-proclaimed "Dead Head" (a fan of the Grateful Dead, a band whose fanbase is known for seeing psychedelic, otherworldly experiences as medicinal for growth and expansion). I should've known right then and there that we were in for a profound experience.

The Twin Flame Pendant and the Matching Tattoo

I found a peculiar pendant on a shelf of the beach house. Its shape was unique but also oddly familiar.

John piped up and said, "That's the shape of your tattoo!"

I had a tattoo on my left forearm of a tribal-like symbol representing Twin Flames, complete with Greg's signature below it. The likelihood that I not only found availability at the beach house but also came across a pendant in the shape of my tattoo is little to none.

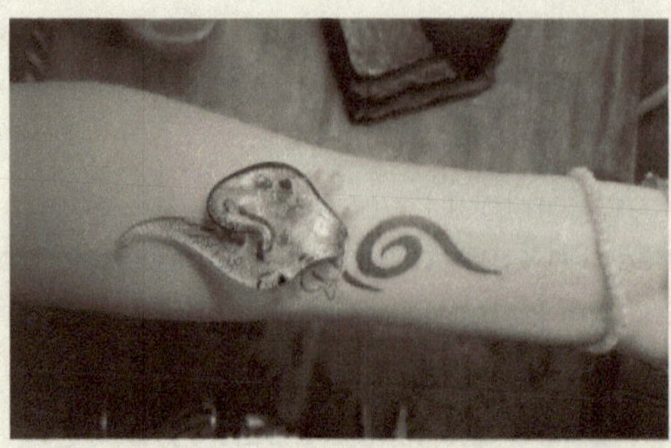

Photo of the pendant (left) next to my tattoo honoring Greg (right). The pendant is a mirror image of the Twin Flame symbol on my tattoo.

The beach trip was pivotal for us. The foundation for our new relationship was being set. Old habits and patterns surfaced so we could purge them. Traits that no longer served us were being shed from our psyche. New memories and special experiences were had, like bathing in the outdoor tub by candlelight surrounded by beautiful orange hibiscus flowers.

We were already bonded at the soul level, but this experience now bonded us at the material level. The trip brought us into alignment with one another so we could come together in harmony. We were now ready to take the next step in our journey.

"I'm Going to Marry You." (Again)

We hadn't been dating for more than a month or two before John looked me in the eyes and said, "I'm going to marry you."

My heart skipped a beat. Not because I was excited and giddy about the idea of marriage but because my late Twin Flame came shining through in that moment.

John said these words with the same conviction and energy. I wanted to chalk it up to coincidence, trying my best not to subconsciously manipulate the situation by relating him to Greg, but the similarity was impossible to dismiss.

Speaking of marriage, we were about to feel what it's like to come together in *alchemical marriage*, also called a soul merge. John and I had only known each other for a brief time, so this experience speaks to the power that a soul connection possess; the power that's realized by coming together on higher levels.

Twin Flame Soul Merge

A soul merge happens when one fully aligns with their Twin Flame. As my guides put it, a soul merge is "the blending of two consciousnesses—two energies living as one." While this occurs at the higher-self level, the partners experience powerful phenomena like physical sensations and out-of-body transcendence.

People who've experienced a soul merge say it's an enriching and empowering feeling. They report things like seeing golden rays of light shooting out from their heart and geometric sunbeams enveloping them. When I saw the golden light in my first meditation, it was symbolic that I was getting into alignment for an alchemical union with my Twin Flame; a signal of the transformation of Greg's higher self passing the torch into another vessel here on Earth.

Soul Merge

Humans can connect on multiple levels. Your aura can connect with another person's aura to transmit information. Your chakras or energy centers can align with theirs in perfect harmony. The frequency you both resonate at mentally, emotionally, and physically can synchronize.

A soul merge, also known as a soul fusion, 5D Union, or alchemical marriage, occurs at the spiritual level. However, it can be felt here at the physical level. The human body attempts to process this 5D marriage using its 3D senses. The result is a reality-bending experience of expansion.

Experiencing the Soul Merge

The soul merge occurred September 10, on what would've been the nineteenth birthday of John's late son, Hunter—yet another example of a significant event occurring on a synchronistic date and time, as if to create an intentional pattern.

The experience was completely unintentional. John and I were lying on his bed, enjoying being in the presence of one another. My daughter was away for the weekend, so my subconscious was more relaxed, relieved of immediate parental responsibility, and able to fully soak up the moment and just *be*. Our minds were in a state of no expectations, with no ego forcing the situation to go in any specific direction.

John was shirtless, and I was wearing a sports bra with my torso exposed. We laid together with skin-on-skin contact at our solar plexus chakra point. This charka is particularly complex. In the body, the solar plexus (or *celiac plexus*) governs the sympathetic nervous system, where not just nerves but millions of *neurons* exist in the gut. As an energy center, the solar plexus is where the silver cord, which connects one's physical body to their higher self and Twin Flame, is tethered. It can respond to the magnetism of your counterpart and cause a sensation known as the "solar plexus pull." Having our solar plexus charka points physically aligned seemed to set things off.

John and I then repositioned our bodies to lie with our sacral (navel) and root (base of the spine) chakras aligned. I felt an electric zap flow through my being and an overwhelming sensation of bliss, like I was wrapped in a warm blanket of love. Again, all of this was unintentional. We weren't aware that the way we were lying corresponded to central energy points!

The physical sensation evolved into a burning, but not painful, energy that radiated from the base of our spines. It pulsated from our tailbones up and down along the spinal column. This is known as Kundalini energy.

In Kundalini, it's like there is an energetic snake that lives coiled up at the base of one's spine. As this energy awakens, the snake uncoils along the spine, sending energetic pulses throughout the body. For some, it takes many months or even years to release this energy intentionally. The power of a higher soul connection surpassed the usual expectations of requiring this training and practice. That power was all we needed to uncoil the snake. It felt like a liquid warmth buzzing at our Root chakra space. There was an unmistakable orgasmic sensation.

From there, we were catapulted to the climax of the soul merge. The shape of reality itself seemed to bend! The perception of our respective selves, one another, and the world exploded into another dimension. Our consciousness expanded and blended into a shared awareness. It defied the single state of consciousness we're told humans are limited to.

I experienced life through his being as if I was him and he was me. I could feel my own hand touching his body and his hand touching me all at once. Things continued to progress from the material world and into the spiritual plane. I'm not sure how to describe it other than saying we were transported to another realm.

The soul merge showed no signs of slowing down. We had no idea what was going on or why it was happening. The only thing I knew for sure was that we were somehow in control of this. I tried to stay grounded in this knowledge and remember that we'd come out of this OK. We stayed there with our eyes closed and reveled in this transcendence for almost two hours.

What Does Being in 5D Union Feel Like?

It felt like everything at once—like a return to home but also like an exploration of a totally new world. All the energy in my being was activated and released to merge with my partner's, resulting in an otherworldly experience that was truly interdimensional. Everything was one: our thoughts, our bodies, our consciousness.

We attained comprehension of the larger "omni-consciousness" or connected consciousness. We were aware of our multidimensional existence as it spanned multiple realities, densities, and states of consciousness all at once.

I remember the experience as being mainly claircognizant, with clairvoyant visuals of another realm. I saw a landscape scene with a big open sky, a green valley that stretched as far as I could see, and large mountains in the distance. This scene didn't stay for long before I entered a realm of pure color and sensation. This prismatic display cohesively formed a peach hue. It looked like all the colors in the universe were being presented simultaneously, existing separately in their own respect but culminating together to create a harmonious peach color.

I thought it was odd that peach, of all colors, was prominent. Wouldn't a bold, striking color like royal blue or divine purple be more appropriate for such a spiritual experience?

Symbology helps explain the presence of this color. Peach is a feminine color that symbolizes vitality, energy, and a sense of playfulness or encouragement. It represents oneness, completion, and wish fulfillment. It signifies the harmony between heaven and Earth—two separate worlds coming together in perfect balance—bringing a sense of peace.

Peach reminds us to focus on maintaining inner peace by staying true to ourselves to live authentically without judgment or distraction from outside forces. (Never allow external events to govern your internal condition.) It encourages us to stay grounded and not get carried away in our fantasies, which can stray us from our inner harmony. Knowing this, it makes a little more sense why peach had such a starring role.

My Twin Flame's interpretation of the soul merge was different from my own but also somehow the same. Here is John's testimony:

"The English language can't do it justice. But if I had to attempt to describe it, I guess I would say that I was experiencing every pleasurable emotion all at the same time. Everything around me became pixelated, and my senses were heightened. When I would feel your skin on mine, the boundaries between the two became blurred and joined each other, and our bodies as well as our minds seemed to meld together. It felt like my senses were overlapping with yours.

Everything was crisp, bright, and vivid, and I remember laughing with a feeling like I was on a roller coaster that was about to go down the first big drop. There was definitely a feeling of anticipation. At the same time, it felt like a two-hour orgasm. It was almost like an explosion, and the roof of my house was torn back and we were stepping out of time. The universe stood still, except for us. The only things that existed were you and me.

Then, I felt like we were in a garden. There was **running water**, beautiful green plants, and flowers. I remember how amazing your body felt in my hands. When I'd slowly trail my hand down your torso, these amazing specs of diamonds and fluorescent dust came off your body. Occasionally, my hand would even pass through you."

Sounds of Water in Transcendental Experiences

Light, love, and water are three fundamental building blocks of life. Many people see light and feel a sense of love, but what about water?

In John's account of the soul merge, he mentions the presence of "running water." Others who've had spiritually transformative experiences also report hearing the sound of water—like a trickling stream, rushing river, or single water droplet. Almost like an indication that the energy was rising and something great was coming.

So, if you ever hear something that sounds like water, but it isn't quite like something you'd hear in this world (when you hear this sound, you'll know), be ready. You may be on the cusp of an ascension experience!

Coming Back to Reality

When we came back to reality from this experience, my partner was shaken, unsure of what had just happened. I'd been through out-of-body experiences, strange paranormal encounters, and a near-death experience that involved "timeline hopping." Nothing compared to this.

John looked at me and asked, "Did you know this was going to happen?".

"No," I replied. "I have no idea what that was!"

What we'd just gone through left us in awe. We had no intention to so much as meditate or daydream, let alone completely depart from this reality and meld together!

Breaking the limits of reality helped us gain reverence for the energetic power our connection could unlock. It instilled a feeling of being destined to be together and that much more was in store for us.

The soul merge speaks to the sheer power of Twin Flames, soul connections, and the expansiveness of our consciousness. And how humans live with such a limited, restricted view of the true nature of our multidimensional existence. The takeaway is that we are each capable of reaching these levels of transcendence.

You can use the power between you and your counterpart to shatter the illusions of reality and access these higher realms. Not only that, but your abilities can be used to help shape the world!

Otherworldly Sex

If the soul merge (a spiritual form of intimacy) can bend our perception of reality, imagine what physical intimacy can do!

Twin Flame sex is "otherworldly," as my late Twin Flame called it. In non-Twin Flame sex, sexual acts can be performed willy-nilly because the individuals aren't bonded by a higher connection between their souls. But Twin Flames share a heightened connection and must be more prudent in their sexual expressions. Their lovemaking is extremely powerful and can have unintended effects like rapid manifestation or mirroring that last long after the act is done. Experienced Twin Flames can use sex as a productive, energetic tool. "With great power comes great responsibility," as they say.

Twin Flame Intimacy

Intimacy isn't restricted to the act of having sex. Let's define what's meant by Twin Flame intimacy:

Twin Flames can show intimacy by the way they think about their partner and the intention they have toward them.

In the eighteen months I was blessed to spend with Greg before he died, he said something that caught me off guard. We were arguing about Lord knows what. He was frustrated and trying to find anything to use as fuel for the fire, when he expressed his frustration that I never touched his member. As he put it, it was like I was repelled by it. I didn't go out of my way to "service" my man. However, he *knew* me. He'd known for over ten years that this wasn't in my sexual repertoire. He didn't complain then, so why'd he bring it up now?

His complaint originated from a disconnect between what he perceived as "normal" intimacy and what we were actually dealing with, which was Twin Flame intimacy. Both Greg and I had unintentionally applied beliefs about sex that we'd gained through experiences outside the Twin Flame connection. What we'd come to expect as "normal" for a healthy sex life from past relationships couldn't be expected for us because *our* sex life had an additional layer of complexity to consider: the energetic effects of our higher soul connection.

While it may be "normal" for the average couple to perform hand play on a regular basis, hand play for Twin Flames is so powerful that it can have energetic ripple effects. To try to put it into words, it's an out-of-this-world sensory overload, physically *and* metaphysically, like a fiery hot key of passion unlocking the floodgates of universal love, and you're swimming in a sea of bliss... all from hand stuff!

When exploring physical intimacy with John, I needed to confirm that he truly was my "new" Twin Flame. I looked at the patterns and trends across both relationships and spotted similarities almost immediately. Things felt the same and were reminiscent of what I'd grown to know as Twin Flame-level intimacy.

For instance, my Twin Flame's primary love language is physical touch. This holds true for both Greg and John, which suggests that a person's preference for giving and receiving love is embedded at a higher level. This part of them is developed from their soul and projected onto their incarnations.

Realizing the higher nature of my Twin Flame's characteristics, traits, and preferences forced me to recognize what that said about *me*—the Twin Flame who mirrors their energy. In this life, I believe my partner's physical preference to express love is designed to help heal my own hang-ups and damage of past trauma regarding sex.

Energy Experiments

While I was aware of the powerful impact Twin Flame sex can have, John had never heard of Twin Flames. At first, he couldn't understand why our intimacy was so... explosive! The best way for him to learn how Twin Flames transcend the rules of "normal" 3D relationships was to have him witness it. And what better way to convey a lasting message to a man than through a positive sexual experience?

The first step to showing John how different Twin Flame sex was involved dissolving any old beliefs of intimacy—the harmful views of what we *think* sex should be and the limiting effect this has. In John's relationship before me, there were themes of watching pornographic content regularly (together, as a couple) and illicit drug use. Years of this reshaped his view of what was normal and expected. Thankfully, it didn't take long for him to rewire this thinking and adjust his behavior. The over-the-top intensity of our supercharged lovemaking and the deep sense of fulfillment it yielded helped to speed this process.

Next, I needed to prove the validity of focusing on energy rather than physicality. I've never used verbal communication during sex; I've never needed it. When John discovered this about me, he didn't believe me. He couldn't understand how I didn't need words to anticipate what he wanted or express what I liked. Moments of heightened energy (like sex) often act as a catalyst for telepathy. Sometimes the telepathic messages would come in so clearly, it startled me to hear someone else's thoughts in my head! It didn't take long for me to show this to John and make him a believer.

With the statement Greg had made to me still lingering in the back of my mind, I started making efforts to fulfill John's needs. This was a big step for me. I broke through the past trauma and made considerable progress to accommodate him. Despite my efforts, John expressed that his need was still not being met. Disappointed and a little embarrassed about having come out of my shell to try to fulfill his desires, it hit me: What if his need wasn't centered around a sexual act? What if his need was *energetic*? That would certainly explain why, of all things, Greg chose to make the complaint he did in our argument many months ago.

Things started making sense when, one evening, John and I had yet another unexpected experience in bed. He asked me to hold his member while we fell asleep. I obliged and grasped it with my hand. Without any movement or stimulation, I felt the excitement build. He reached over and began to return the favor. The pleasure from his gentle stroking grew too incredible, and I released this energy by making slow, subtle movements with my hand. I was barely moving my hand at all, but the pleasure it produced was like we were sixteen-year-old kids on MDMA when really, we were middle-aged adults who were exhausted after a long day.

Something wasn't adding up; the physical effort didn't match the huge energetic payout. Our bodies were doing one thing while our inner selves and dimensional layers, chakras, and consciousness were doing something completely different. How could we feel such high energy from such minimal activity?

When it seemed like things couldn't get any more intense, the ample energy we were building activated. Things turned from simple touching to something otherworldly, unbelievable, without changing what we were physically doing. No going faster or harder. The moment was so powerful, the overwhelming burst of mental, spiritual, emotional, and physical energy led to a simultaneous climax.

Not quite sure how to process what had just happened, John reacted with single words and broken sentences, awe-struck by what had transpired. Our minds had trouble processing the incredible sensations we experienced and couldn't make sense of how such a grand finale was possible.

This wasn't the first time that the intensity of the act performed didn't match the level of energy it produced. There were times when John would touch me like any other man touches a woman, and my whole body quivered in ecstasy, as if the Divine Himself was touching me. The energy has been so intense and the vibration so high that I've felt a buzzing sensation in the space between my eyes, right near the third eye chakra. It felt like the invisible threads that connected us were activating and buzzing with stimulation.

These heightened experiences occurred whenever I consciously flowed energy into my touch. In my mind's eye, I'd focus on the love I have for my partner, and with a deep appreciation for who they are at the purest level, I let this flow from my heart out through my body to them.

These energy experiments helped reveal the missing piece of information I needed: the concerns I'd heard from both partners about their needs going unfulfilled (despite a larger-than-life sex life) were the result of the misinterpretation or misdirection of energy. I also confirmed that channeling Twin Flame energy was the key to creating Earth-shattering moments in bed.

Chapter 15

Connecting the Dots

As my relationship with John developed, I continued to work with my guides every day. They were very supportive of our union. But I still struggled to get any real information about who John was to me. I'd ask my guides questions in meditation like, "Why can't I get any background info on John?" And get answers like, "Because [Greg and John] are the same. They are distant fragments of the same monad, rooted in the same overarching soul energy."

The interactions with my guides and with others who were connected to my Twin Flame journey continued to develop and eventually validate Greg as my miracle incarnate.

Always on His Side

Like most couples, John and I encountered moments where our personalities clashed. I'd be irked by something like his dirty socks strewn across the bedroom floor when the laundry bin is two feet away. My ego would try to keep me frustrated and distant, but my guides encouraged a different direction. As their helper, Greg often chimed in via my inner dialogue to assist.

One time, I was huffing and puffing over something trivial— so trivial, I forget what it was. Greg came through with words of wisdom to "get over it" and advised me to go over and give John a hug. In my mind's eye, I jokingly gave Greg a hard time about how he was "on John's side."

If Greg were alive with his ego intact, there's no way he'd ever cheer me on to be with another man. Then again, maybe I'm not giving him enough credit. Maybe my own assumptions about how he'd act were what boxed him in and manifested in his behavior. So, I did my best to release my opinions of how I thought Greg *should* behave and created space for him to show me how he would behave.

Focused on how I'd lost Greg and how, in the face of that, staying mad at John for trivial things was silly, I obliged to the advice. I figured, why not listen to this intuitive guidance? I was interested to see if following this guidance would really keep me on a higher path.

I took a moment to get over myself, walked into the bedroom where John was, and gave him a huge hug—and was sure to mean it. Sure enough, it defused the situation. It proved that my guides truly do have my best interests at heart.

Another time, I was taking John's clothes out of the dryer after a long workday. Laundry was the *last* thing I wanted to be doing. Stress at work had me in a state far removed from the spiritual closeness I can usually feel. So when Greg came through in that moment, the energetic disturbance gave me a slight headache. I was resonating at too low a frequency to receive higher messages seamlessly.

I recognized Greg's energy and playfully asked, "What now?"

He offered me a piece of advice: "You can be a lot to handle, so try not to be your *full* self. You have to be the bigger person and choose your battles this time, which will help John come into himself."

Again, it seemed like Greg was always on John's side! This was a silly thought, though, because truly, Greg was on the side of me living my highest path, my best life.

Seeing the Links

Greg's Spirit became more active in getting me to see the links between him and John. For instance, another time, I was in the other room when John called to me, "Baby." There was a strong infliction on the "bay" part, almost singsong, like "bay-bee." It stopped me right where I stood. It was phonetically the same way Greg would say, "Come here." These two phrases from these two men had the same unique vocal pattern.

Then, Greg asked in my mind's eye, "How does he *feel* to you?" I took a moment to take inventory.

"He feels like... *you!*" I exclaimed.

A person's love has a unique energy signature. When that signature matches perfectly across two individuals, chances are you're dealing with two people of the same soul energy. The way John's energy felt and how it perfectly intertwined with mine was the same as it was with Greg.

The more involved I got with John, the more apparent it was that he was my miracle manifested. Of course, I'm only human, and despite having physical proof, my mental mind still craved additional confirmation to wrap my head around the idea.

Curious to see what else would be revealed, I asked, "Can I have more confirmation?"

Greg replied, "Have you looked into his eyes... I mean, *really* looked?"

I gasped when I realized, "No, I haven't!"

I went into the bedroom where John was resting. I knew it might be awkward for me to randomly gaze into his eyes, so I prefaced what I was about to do by saying, "Bear with me. This might be weird, but I need to see something."

I sat on the bed beside him and stared into his green eyes. I wasn't sure exactly what I was looking for but knew that I'd recognize it when I saw it. A minute or so passed, and there it was! I don't know how to explain it. It was something subtle and indescribable. I felt a feeling of absolute truth. I recognized my Twin Flame, sure as day.

Interpersonal Relationships

The relationships with people outside my Twin Flame connection add another layer of meaning. These relationships acted like embeddings, an AI concept that adds contextual meaning to a subject so it can be understood multidimensionally. A simple definition of a word won't suffice to make sense of something. A network of understanding is required to describe it fully. This is how the other relationships in my life worked to create a deeper understanding of my Twin Flame journey. They portrayed a greater network of entanglement with myself (and consequently, with my Twin Flame), my life, and my soul.

Connection: Frauke

I kept in touch with Greg's mother, a German woman named Frauke. She and I didn't talk much before he died, though he always wanted us to be close. While some would've been quick to dismiss deep discussions with a grieving mother due to the emotional heaviness of it all, I welcomed it. Greg had been her pillar of strength during the storms of life. I wanted her to feel as much love as possible and not feel alone.

Frauke is a woman of logic. She doesn't believe in God, which is painful to imagine a parent mourning the loss of a child, thinking that after they die, they've faded into nothingness. At first, I was scared to bring up the spiritual phenomena I was experiencing. I had no way to physically prove beyond reasonable doubt that any of it was true (did I mention she's an attorney?). I feared she'd think I was saying these whimsical, fantasy things to cheer her up, or she'd become upset that I still felt so connected to him when she felt so far.

I asked Greg's higher self how to handle this. "How can I best help your mother through this time?"

He replied, "Don't. I got it. There are plans for her."

I was disappointed. I felt powerless to help her. It was clear from Spirit that it wasn't my place, so I obliged and limited my interactions to only what I felt intuitively guided to do. But one day, the urge to freely express myself became too much. My heart was screaming at me to share all these amazing things I was experiencing with her son.

To my surprise, Frauke welcomed my remarks. She saw the conviction in my claims even through the limited communication of text messaging. My story provided hope for her of life beyond death. She started to open up to the world's magic. I was tickled pink when one day, she embraced the idea of belief and said, "Maybe spirits *can* influence our thinking." It was groundbreaking! Just as this was a journey of awakening and transformation for me, this was also Greg's mother's journey to open her heart.

My relationship with Frauke also gave me the painful insight into what it's like to lose a child. While I was happy to give her a shoulder to cry on in hopes it would help her grieve, there was another purpose for our discussions. John had lost his newborn son many years ago and never got to know his child. Frauke was blessed to have three decades with Greg; and to learn who this miraculous soul, her child, was. Never having lost a child myself, this contrast gave me perspective to transform my sympathy for John's loss into empathy.

As one of many embeddings in my Twin Flame journey network, the connection to Frauke is full of purpose and meaning.

Intersection of the Inner Child

Like many new mothers, Frauke was ecstatic about her new bundle of joy when Greg was born. She took photos and documented his early years and, after his death, she poured over them to mourn him. Her trip down memory lane to Greg's childhood coincided with an important point of my spiritual development: healing the inner child.

Inner Child

You carry your inner child with you from childhood. It's the part of you that's innocent, playful, and full of wonder, even when the woes of the real world harden your adult self. It's also the part of you that's been hurt, neglected, or abandoned in some way.

Healing your inner child is essential for spiritual development. The healing process involves acknowledging your pain, forgiving yourself and others, and learning to love and accept yourself universally. This unlocks your natural curiosity about the world and gives you an open mind to explore new possibilities. The self-discovery gained from healing your inner child leads to a complete, more fulfilling life.

The topic of inner child healing kept appearing in my research, in conversations with friends, and social media. These were Spirit's hints to address it. Knowing better than to ignore Spirit's suggestion, I lay down to meditate in an unguided session and let my guides take the wheel.

My third eye activated, and I saw a vision of Little Me, about six years old, standing on a big theater stage. The room was totally dark except for a spotlight shining on me overhead. I remembered the eager curiosity this age brings and the vulnerability of being so green. My adult self felt an instinct to protect my inner child's pure state. This was overpowered by my longing for the innocence my inner child exuded. I was sad, thinking I'd never have that innocence again. Then, I realized I *was* that innocence! I've had it all along. It was my *choice* to let the world harden my heart, to comply with the illusion that adulthood strips us of this beautifully expansive state. It is my *choice* to soften it.

After this one-on-one moment with my inner child, a second spotlight flipped on to reveal Little Greg standing a few feet downstage. It never occurred to me to wonder what it'd be like if we knew one another as children. Would we play together? Would we even notice one another?

There, standing before me, were the inner children who Greg and I had forgotten. Our inner children were finally reunited—his to his existence in Spirit and mine to my adult self here. We stood side-by-side in all our unburdened purity. Little Greg looked over at Little Me and smiled, but Little Me was bashful. She didn't know who this boy was. Greg's presence had a comfort to it, a comfort that I recognized from knowing him in adulthood, and Little Me started to let her guard down to this stranger. Little Me and Little Greg bonded, transforming our past, current, and projected unity across incarnations.

I felt I'd accomplished what Spirit wanted me to do. Healing my inner child and meeting Greg's were big steps. I thought that was it. Leave it to Spirit to keep the surprises coming because a few days later, I learned the real reason behind all this inner child hype.

Greg's First Friend

It'd been a few months since I'd talked to Frauke when my phone lit up with a text message. She said she was going through old photos and notes from when Greg was little and found something of interest.

On September 24, 1988, Frauke journaled about one-and-a-half-year-old Gregory. He loved to laugh and play on his tricycle. He was a quiet child and didn't begin speaking at the expected age. His bilingual German-English upbringing might've delayed his verbal development. Or perhaps he just liked observing. Either way, when baby Greg made the effort to pipe up and speak, his words were especially cherished.

Greg was playing that day when he turned to his mother and said, "Lisa." This occurred six months and two days before I was born, so at first, I was confused. Was there a glitch in the matrix? Did I exist in a parallel universe in 1988 but was caught in a Mandela Effect and born in 1989 in this one?

Frauke explained that baby Greg's first friend was a girl around his age named Lisa. Relieved that I didn't need to worry about a secondary existence or that reality was folding in on itself, I was in awe of this "coincidence." For soft-spoken baby Greg to use his rare words to say the name of his little friend—to say *my* name—is beautiful. For Frauke to find this note and be impacted by it enough to pick up the phone and text me is beautiful. For me to receive her message just days after I completed the inner child meditation was beyond beautiful... it was fate.

Not only were our inner children metaphysically bonded in the meditation, but now there was evidence of a material, physical connection. Though I wasn't born yet, the universe was sprinkling in synchronicities—little hints to illuminate Greg's life path—which would be identified decades later as meaningful points of connection. Greg was born into the world with a girl named Lisa, and he left the world with a girl named Lisa.

The date of Frauke's journal entry, September 24, boded even more themes of connection. Everyone significant in my life can point to a critical life event on September twenty-something (more on this later). To tie this back to this journey of rebirth: John's infant son, Hunter, departed this world in that late September time frame.

Connection: Hunter

Though he was only on Earth for a handful of weeks, John's son, Hunter, played an active role in this journey. He appeared to me in meditation before I knew John had lost a son.

In the early morning hours of July 13, 2021, about a week before I met John, I lay down to meditate. This was around the time of my intention setting. I conveyed my intention via meditation and journaled to solidify the following:

> *I want to rebirth our Twin Flame connection. I want to put in the time and effort to get to the surrender stage with you. I want all the things we used to dream about... because they're already ours. I just need you here with me to achieve them. Like you said: "The universe always puts us back together—always."*
>
> *I'm ready to evolve our bond and rebirth it into what we both know it can be. We've both seen the pure, raw heart of it. I know you love me. Let me show you I love you. Let's transcend time and space. Let's love fearlessly. Let's face this world hand in hand, together. Let's focus on what really matters. Let's surrender to our bond and be the power couple we were always meant to be.*
>
> *We were never given the chance to be together when both of us were ready. Now, we finally are. I know it's not too late. I know I'll find you again. Our hearts are always connected. Find your way back to me, Love.*
>
> *Love,*
> *Your Squeaker*

Later that day, I meditated again at 3:17 p.m. and was shown a vision of an individual I couldn't place. I only saw his face but could make out the details of his eyes, smile, and hair. He had a youthful, childlike appearance. It was a young boy. He had short, light-brown hair, a determined look in his eye, and a quirked smile. There was a mischievous look to him, but his energy was good-willed. I've never had a person I don't know come in so clearly before. I sketched his face in my journal and left it at that, unsure how to figure out who he was.

Not long after, I met John. It took a few weeks for it to dawn on me: he had a striking resemblance to the boy from my meditation! I shrugged it off as having seen a premonition of John, which was impressive but not as wild as the vision's true meaning.

As we were getting to know one another, John shared a heartbreaking detail with me. He had a son named Hunter, who died after a few short weeks from a heart condition.

At the risk of sounding crazy, I told John that I believed the boy in my meditation was Hunter. It was farfetched to think that I could not only visualize someone who looked like John before I met him but that I could feel their energy and how similar it was to John's, too. He was skeptical but didn't shut the idea down entirely.

On a particularly spiritually active day, I had a hunch to ask John for a photo of Hunter's mother. John obliged, and the second I laid eyes on the picture of this beautiful red-headed woman, I instantly knew that the boy I saw was Hunter. I was floored, but unsure of how to tell John that I was convinced I'd seen his dead son in meditation—the son he mourned, the son he never had the chance to know.

I presented the evidence of why I believed this, including how Hunter visually appeared, the impression I got from him, and my interpretation of his demeanor. Though John never got to know his son, he seemed to have that fatherly instinct of how his child's personality would've been. And it aligned with what I described.

John accepted my claim that it was Hunter in my vision. This was further proof that John was meant to walk this path with me.

Connection: Ryan and Jeff

In my research for this book, I reviewed my old journals to form a timeline of events and uncovered a direct intersection of my Twin Flame's life paths. On August 12, John's forty-first birthday, another embedding surfaced—a point of connection between John and Greg.

The journal entry was from 2010. I wrote how Greg wasn't being himself and acting like he was hiding something. Feeling that I couldn't trust him, I broke up with him. He called me a day or two later in a state of hysteria. He was yelling and crying so hard he could barely breathe. His voice was filled with intense desperation and pain. He was breaking down more and more by the second. I kept asking him, "What's wrong?" I finally got an answer: "Today is the anniversary of Ryan's death."

He went on to share a deep, dark secret he'd been harboring about an event that happened nine years earlier. As Greg told the story, back in the early 2000s, when he was fourteen to sixteen years old, he fell in with a crowd of guys who were in their early twenties. They lived on the opposite side of town, which might as well have been Siberia for a fourteen-year-old with no driver's license. So it's odd that they met in the first place.

When the group got together, they'd get into shenanigans unfitting for a fourteen-year-old, including doing IV drugs like heroin. The two people he admired the most in this group of friends were Ryan and Jeff. One night while they were out partying, Ryan accidentally overdosed. The group was unsure what to do for their friend. They panicked and started throwing out crazy ideas like burying him in the woods near an overpass—a frivolous idea that was obviously fueled by panic and immaturity.

In fight-or-flight mode, they walked through the forest with this plan for what felt like hours, petrified about what was taking place. Greg shocked me when he said, they actually found a spot and started digging. As he told me this, he was on the verge of a complete breakdown, distraught and frantic over the intense emotion he'd held for the last nine years.

He believed they really did bury someone that night, but I had trouble buying it. Greg had been known to tell these big, bad stories about how rough and tough he was, but that wasn't who he was. His heart was too sensitive for his tale to be true.

Something about the story was true, though, as evidenced by the emotional impact it had on him. I asked his ex-girlfriend if she knew anything about the Ryan and Jeff story. She claimed that both men were alive and well. One had moved to a state up north, and another settled down locally to start a family.

I wasn't sure what to believe. Who were Ryan and Jeff? Did someone die that night? Was what Greg said true? Today, Greg is no longer with us clarify. But my new connection with John might yield some answers.

Talking with John one night, I casually mentioned that Greg had a friend named Ryan years ago. John joked, "Wouldn't it be funny if that was the same Ryan I know?"

I went on to explain that Greg's story also involved a person named Jeff. John surprised me when he shared that him and Ryan had a third friend they hung out with back then who'd moved out of state. This friend's name was Jeff. He added that while Jeff was no longer in the area, Ryan lived in town with his wife and children... exactly as Greg's ex-girlfriend said.

Could John's Ryan and Jeff be the same people Greg had fallen in with all those years ago? They were the right age and originated from the part of town Greg shared in his story. If they were the same people, it'd draw a tangible connection between John and Greg—a direct overlap in their lives that connected the dots between them.

Proof Through Synchronicities

I was driving across town, using talk-to-text to message John to see if he'd asked his friend Ryan if he remembered Greg. I was focused on my message to John, so I didn't notice the scenery passing me along the way. I looked around and realized I was passing the overpass and lake Greg referenced in the story. Then, I received incoming texts from Greg's mom who was feeling nostalgic. Unaware of my mission to fill in the blanks of the Ryan and

Jeff story, she sent me photos of Greg from that time. As if that wasn't enough, a song by mewithoutYou was playing over Bluetooth. mewithoutYou's music was pivotal in my relationship with Greg. Their music is known for its lyrical poetry and their ability to intertwine love, faith, and complexities of life into their songs. Coincidentally, that band had just played their final show four days before—the end of an era.

I stopped at an intersection when I looked up, only to see the same model year of Greg's beloved truck that his mother fixed up in his memory. I kept driving and the words on a street sign jumped out at me: "Tanner St." Tanner was a friend of mine in college, born the day before me, who passed away many years ago and had been a point of contention between me and Greg.

So many signs packed into just a few moments—it was like the universe was just throwing synchronicities at me by this point! Whether they were from spiritual forces like Greg trying to get my attention or occurrences through the natural fabric of the universe, the significance of these signs is profound.

To add to the Ryan and Jeff connection, the date of the tragic incident Greg described occurred on September 29 in the early 2000s. John lost his infant son on September 19, 2002. My ex-husband lost his youngest brother to suicide on September 28, 2011. When I realized the significance that this period in September held, I was floored.

I was determined to understand the link between these people and their losses. There was something significant, an important message was waiting to be surfaced. I could feel it! As I was going through the various leads to identify the links between them, Greg came through and suggested, "Add up the numbers in the dates."

Sure enough, the numerology of the dates aligned:

September 29, 2001—R.I.P. Ryan   23

September 19, 2002—R.I.P. Hunter   23

(I couldn't help but chuckle that the dates reduced to 23, a number that inspired the 2007 film "The Number 23" starring Jim Carrey, where the main character finds a novel about the mysterious meaning of the number 23 only to discover that he was a schizophrenic who had repressed his obsession with 23. This was a favorite movie of Greg and mine.)

These individuals played critical roles in shaping our lives. Beyond that, the timing of events in our lives also exhibited similar patterns that make one question whether we're mere subjects of the random, chaotic universe or if there is a greater thread of divine timing at play. Whether talking about the 3D physical realm or the 5D spiritual world, both are subject to the 4D: Time. What gives something meaning? Having synchronicities in the names of people you know or significant dates of life events doesn't necessarily carry meaning. Everything is relative to *time*.

Connection: Pop Culture

The first episode in the season of the TV Show, *It's Always Sunny in Philadelphia* TV that aired in 2019 featured a couple named Lisa and Greg. I've never heard "Lisa and Greg" used in a TV show or movie before. The timing of when it aired is peculiar, as well. The original air date was September 25, 2019, a few months after Greg re-entered my life (there goes that week in September again).

In the show, the main characters host an Airbnb where Lisa and Greg end up staying. The couple is distraught and arguing, and the main cast suspects it's because one of them has a secret romantic lover. It turns out the arguments the gang overheard were about Lisa and Greg's emotional strain of losing their son. At the time, this didn't hold any meaning, but leave it to the universe for everything to fall into place in divine timing. Once I met John, who'd lost his son, things made sense.

Another pop culture connection is found in the FX television show *What We Do In The Shadows,* a satirical comedy about a family of vampires. It was one of Greg's favorite shows. I can almost hear his voice when I remember him remarking how funny the show was. It wasn't until a year and a half after he died that I realized the show has a significant parallel to us.

In season one, vampire Nadja finds her lover, Gregor, who has been reincarnated as a man named Jeff. When writing this book, I toyed with using alternate names for people. Greg would've been Alan. John would've been Jeff. To notice that the show that Greg so adamantly pitched to me features a lead female vampire finding her love interest incarnated into this lifetime again as Jeff, the name I was going to use to refer to my new Twin Flame in this book... it's mind-blowing.

Nadja describes her relationship with Gregor as one of high-intensity sexual energy, much ravaging, and passion. She devoutly believes that she has found Gregor again in Jeff, and they declare, "We have defeated even time itself." The irony is that after finding Jeff and activating Gregor's energy within him, Nadja leaves him to tend to her husband. In other words, she has this intense soul connection that always keeps her coming back, and she knows she will always be reunited with Gregor, but chooses to spend her life in marriage with someone else. The parallels to how things went down in my life are uncanny!

The End of an Era

About a year after meeting John, multiple endings occurred back-to-back. I'd just undergone a massive personal transformation. Now, life was transforming itself, too. It brought old themes and patterns to an end so that greater, higher ones could emerge. Everything was resetting, closing out, and setting the stage for the next cycle.

To explain, I need to backtrack a little. I entertained the idea of dating other people in the fall of 2020 when Greg was away, and I tried an online dating app. I was bombarded with pointless banter and conversations with people who lacked substance or didn't know themselves well enough to be authentic. But my conversations continued with one individual. We didn't talk really at the romantic level. We debated things like economic theories and cryptocurrency. My connection to this person eventually faded, but just three weeks before Greg's death, I received a special gift from them: knowledge of the band Starset.

This band's music would carry me through the darkest moments of grieving Greg's passing. Starset's music tells a thought-provoking story of love, loss, and looking out into the universe to hold onto the connection that's still there. The lyrics of their songs were too perfect, as if their music was written for Twin Flames.

Starset announced an East Coast tour in 2021. The closest concert was a three-and-a-half-hour drive away in late June—the same time of year I'd first met Greg many years ago. Despite the distance, time, and cost of a hotel, I felt compelled to make it to the show. It signified the "end of an era," like a material symbolization of concluding this stage in the cycle of rebirth. The Starset show was the perfect occasion to serve as the ritual to conclude the previous period of my life.

Then, my all-time favorite band, mewithoutYou, who held even more meaning to me and my relationship with Greg, announced their final tour. I saw mewithoutYou's final North Carolina performance in early June. There's more tied into the mewithoutYou show, too, like how my best friend, who passed away three months later and was also intertwined with Greg, randomly ended up venturing out to the concert with me. It was one of the last times I saw them alive and gives yet another meaning to the phrase "the end of an era."

John experienced a major "end of an era" moment in his life, too. The ex-girlfriend he'd shared an on-again, off-again five-year relationship with got into trouble—long-term legal trouble. While John attempted to find a more righteous path, this girl had chosen a less wholesome one. Sadly, she was caught up in the world of easy living and drugs. To make an extra buck, she allegedly sold two people a drug that turned out to be fentanyl. Their doses were lethal, and the girl was arrested for death by distribution.

Until that point, John had trouble cutting her out of his life. She'd call at obscene hours of the night, fighting with her boyfriend and calling John to come to her emotional rescue. She tugged on his heartstrings, and he had a hard time ignoring her pleas for help. Now that she was in jail for the foreseeable future, he could conclude that part of his life was officially over. He could begin to heal. It was divine timing.

In one of the final endings, the historic theater that hosted the weekly viewing of *The Rocky Horror Picture Show* closed its doors. It had been a state landmark since the 1940s, but the owner decided to retire and suspended the theater's operations. *The Rocky Horror Picture Show* was near and dear to my heart. It was the Friday night stomping ground for Greg and my circle of friends before I knew who he was. In our later years, Greg and I indulged our nostalgia and attended the show together.

On August 26 (8/26, a date that's always stood out to me), the theater held one final showing of *The Rocky Horror Picture Show*. It was a sold-out affair. This final performance was just in time for me to show John that part of my world. It was the perfect finale for the "end of an era."

The transformation into a new cycle was complete.

# Chapter 16

A New Chapter

I'll never forget the night I was lying in bed with my new counterpart when my late Twin Flame suddenly came through to me and said, "You can call on their higher self now." This was confirmation that it was finally time; I'd reached the point where John could fully assume the role of my Twin Flame.

Bringing about the miracle of rebirth took much time and effort. It required a total commitment to transformation and growth. Of course, there were struggles and pitfalls along the way, but the reward was so worth it. Finding the person to continue my Twin Flame relationship with was not the reward. The reward was something so much more.

The reward was catapulting my growth into my identity as a spiritually guided lightworker, so I can fulfill my soul's purpose of teaching and helping others. I was able to harness the effects of losing Greg in a positive way. I spiritually awakened and learned how to live *with* life. I entered co-creator mode and was empowered to see the messages, signs, and synchronicities to help me navigate life's current. I became enlightened about myself, realizing the deeper truths and alchemizing things that no longer served me.

I've reached new heights in my social, familial, and professional lives as well as my romantic one, all because I took this expanded journey of rebirth, a journey of getting to know Spirit and focusing on the subtle, metaphysical aspects of human existence that brought me to worlds I never thought possible.

I've activated my purpose of helping others see the patterns of connection in their lives and detect the meaningful embeddings to drive them. This is how I'm aiding the mass spiritual awakening that's taking place. If you've read this book, you have a similar purpose.

A Purposeful Love Story

The journey of rebirth was not simply about calling Greg's "walk-in" soul into my life. The rebirth pertained to multiple levels, including a rebirth of how I saw Greg—a transformation of our relationship from one of lovers to one of a much higher purpose. It was a rebirth of my own self and an awakening to view life with an expanded consciousness. It was also a rebirth of my Twin Flame connection to carry on our mission.

I was blessed to find John, who resonated the same Twin Flame energy as Greg, so we could carry out our mission to aid humanity's ascension, continue our soul's journey, and amplify our development.

The journey from grief to rebirth was monumental, but it was not the final stage. The way this story ends is still unwritten, because we always have the choice of how we choose to live our lives. I could choose to embrace the person my late love has sent me and continue down this path. Or I could take the lessons I've learned, focus on myself, and perhaps encounter another "walk-in" soul later down the road. Either way, I will continue to regard the interconnected nature of life and use its cues to guide my journey.

This story is a reminder that we are always connected, always supported, and always able to hear the inaudible drum beat of life's rhythm. You are part of an entangled network of souls who use their energy to support a productive, uplifting life for you.

In a time of AI and the dawn of the Age of Aquarius, we don't need to turn to apps or mechanics for fulfillment. All the information we need is being transmitted to us in the ether and transcribed in the depths of our hearts. This information holds the key to making possible the impossible. And we are all capable of interpreting it. *That* is the lesson.

As a wise man once said, *"The universe always puts us back together. Always."*

Bibliography

"Heart Chakra," AnthroWiki, last modified June 2, 2021, 06:14, https://en.anthro.wiki/Heart_chakra

McCraty, Rollin. 2004. "The Energetic Heart: Bioelectromagnetic Interactions Within and Between People." Institute of HeartMath Institute. https://www.heartmath.org/research/research-library/energetics/energetic-heart-bioelectromagnetic-communication-within-and-between-people/.2003

Rubik, Beverly, David Muehsam, Richard Hammerschlag, and Shamini Jain. 2015. "Biofield Science and Healing: History, Terminology, and Concepts." *Global Advances in Health and Medicine* 4 (1_suppl): gahmj.2015.038. https://doi.org/10.7453/gahmj.2015.038.suppl

Vision Train, *Vision Train Website,* accessed November 11, 2022. https://www.visiontrain.org/

About the Author

Lisa C. Arrington

Lisa C. Arrington is a writer, believer, and mother from Raleigh-Durham, North Carolina. She shares lessons from her near-death experience and the spiritual transformation that occurred after her the passing of her Twin Flame sparked an awakening in 2021.

Lisa earned a B.S. in Business Management—Marketing with an economics minor from the University of North Carolina at Charlotte. She built her professional career as an enterprise search engine optimization (SEO) manager.

After completing a decade-long study of Biblical scripture with pastor Jason Stone, Lisa studied spirit communication under the mentorship of medium Deborah Richmond Foulkes. She continues to study the power of soul connection, embeddings, and entanglement in one's life and seeks to bridge concepts of frequency, energy, and vibration to help others understand the world around them.

She founded the Twin Flames and Soulmates Grief Support group to help others and publishes related information on her blog, *https://etherealsoul.net/*.